D1220398

2000s

Ten Years of Popular Hits Arranged for **EASY PIANO**

Arranged by Dan Coates

DECADE *by* DECADE

Alfred

Produced by
Alfred Music Publishing Co., Inc.
P.O. Box 10003
Van Nuys, CA 91410-0003
alfred.com

Printed in USA.

ISBN-10: 0-7390-5177-6
ISBN-13: 978-0-7390-5177-1

Cover photo: © istockphoto/davidforeman

Contents

BECAUSE OF YOU

In September of 2002, Kelly Clarkson won the first season of American Idol, Fox's smash hit singing competition. Following her victory, Clarkson began a successful performing and recording career. She co-wrote "Because of You"—the certified-platinum single from her second album, *Breakaway*—with David Hodges and Ben Moody (two former members of the Grammy-winning rock band Evanescence.)

Words and Music by
Kelly Clarkson, Ben Moody and David Hodges
Arranged by Dan Coates

Verse 2:
I lose my way,
And it's not too long before you point it out.
I cannot cry,
Because I know that's weakness in your eyes.
I'm forced to fake a smile,
A laugh, every day of my life.
My heart can't possibly break
When it wasn't even whole to start with.
(To Chorus:)

BREAKAWAY

This Kelly Clarkson hit single made its debut appearance in the 2004 film *The Princess Diaries 2: Royal Engagement.* After its chart-topping success, "Breakaway" was included on Clarkson's second studio album of the same name. The album won the 2006 Grammy for Best Pop Vocal Album.

Words and Music by
Matthew Gerrard, Bridget Benenate and Avril Lavigne
Arranged by Dan Coates

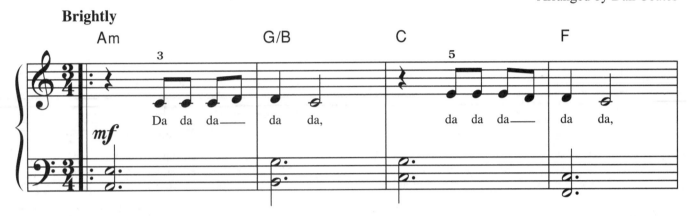

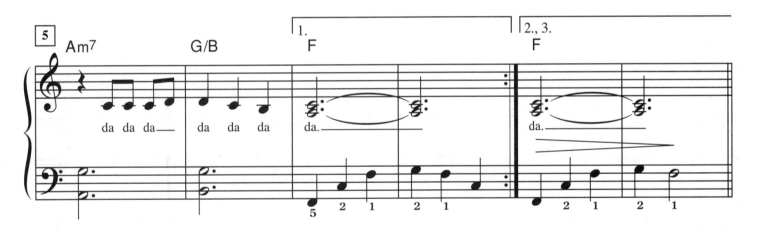

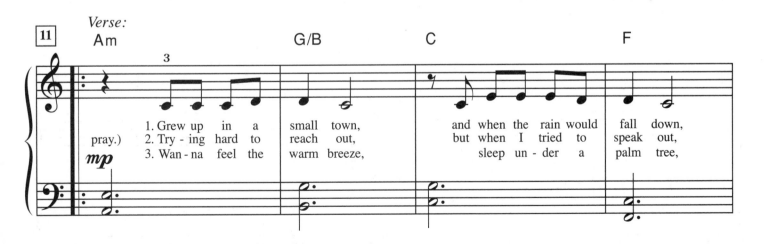

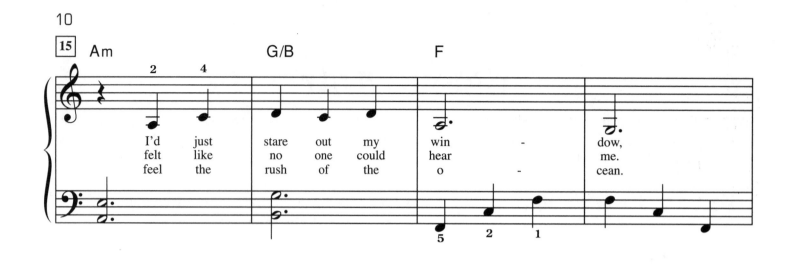

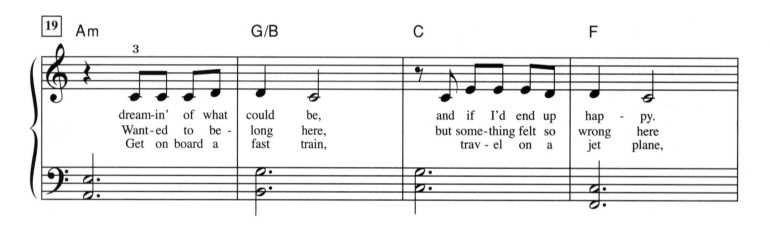

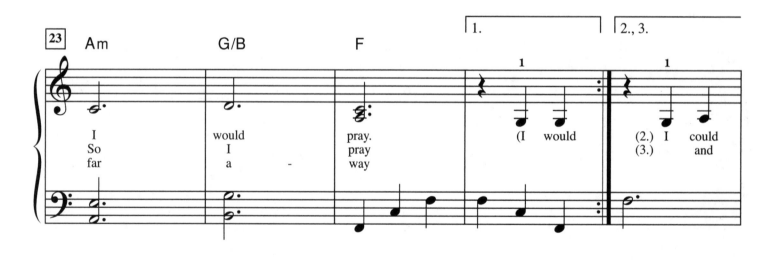

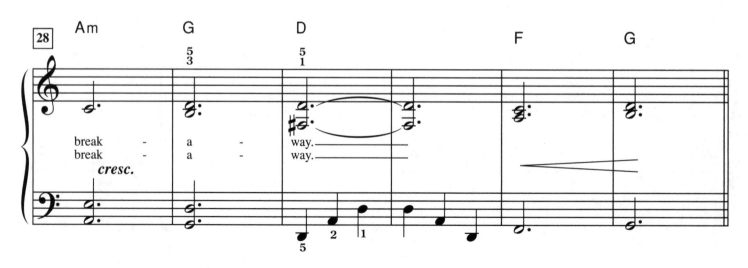

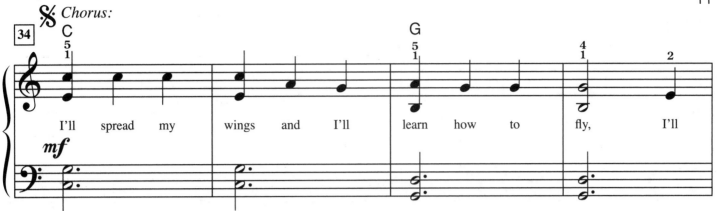

%. *Chorus:*

I'll spread my wings and I'll learn how to fly, I'll

(2.) do what it takes——— 'til I touch the sky. And I'll make a wish,
(3.) Though it's not eas - y to tell you good - bye, got - ta take a risk,

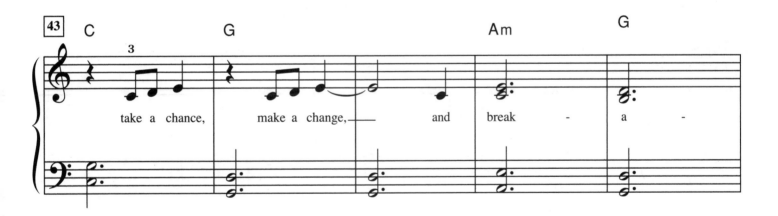

take a chance, make a change,——— and break - a -

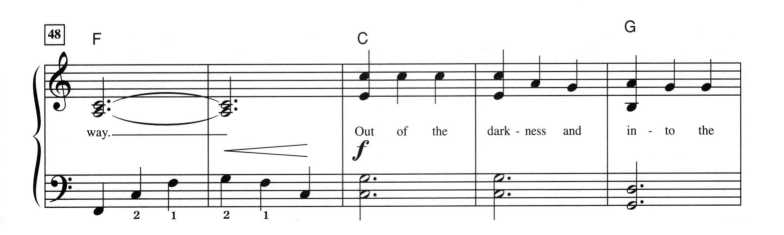

way.——— Out of the dark - ness and in - to the

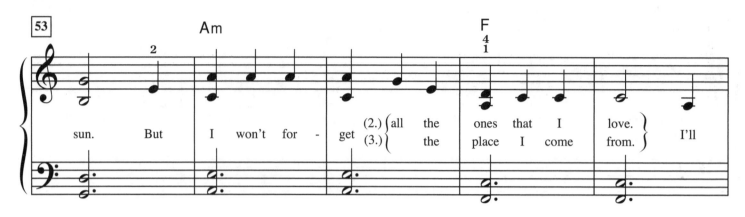

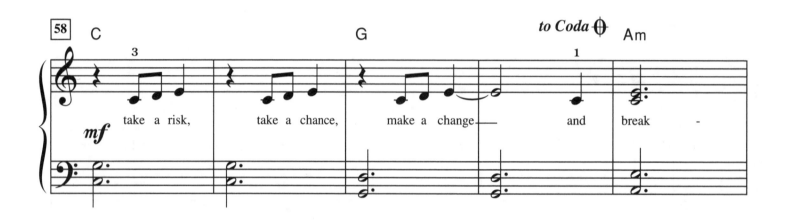

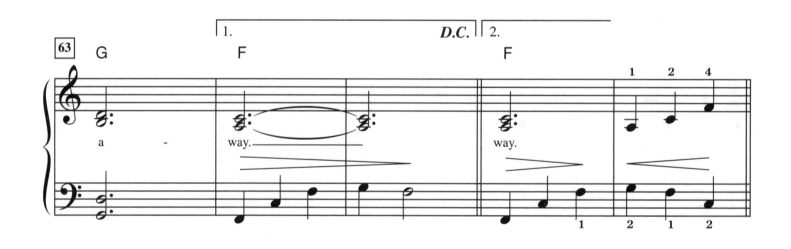

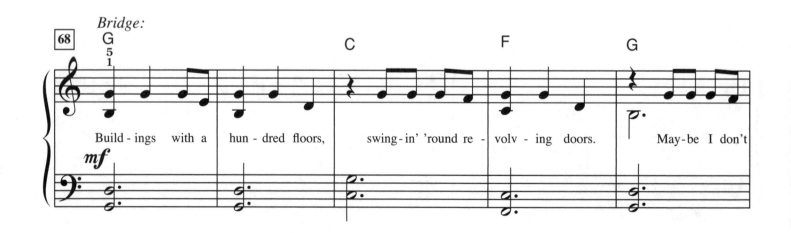

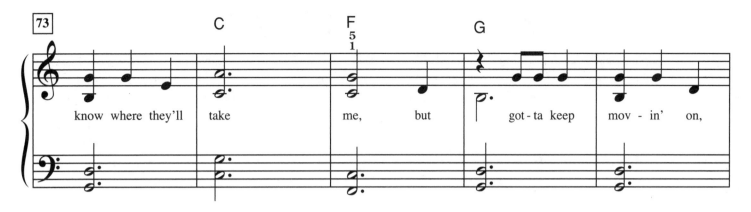

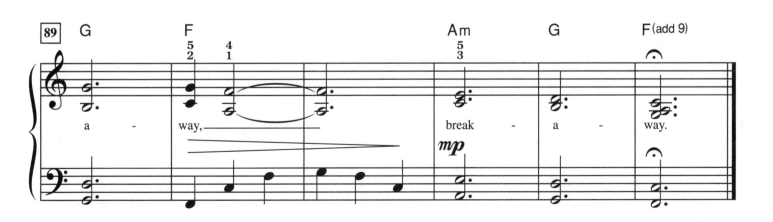

BEFORE HE CHEATS

Carrie Underwood, winner of American Idol season 4, had a megahit with this single from her debut album, *Some Hearts,* in 2006. The vivid lyrics tell the story of a woman who seeks revenge on her unfaithful boyfriend. In addition to holding spots on the country, adult contemporary and pop charts, it was named Single of the Year by the Country Music Association in 2007.

Words and Music by Josh Kear and Chris Tompkins
Arranged by Dan Coates

BELIEVE
(FROM "THE POLAR EXPRESS")

The 2004 Academy award-nominated film *The Polar Express* was based on the 1986 children's book of the same name by Chris Van Allsburg. "Believe," sung by Josh Groban and featured in various scenes throughout the movie, was nominated for Best Original Song at the Academy Awards and won a Grammy award in 2006.

Words and Music by Alan Silvestri and Glen Ballard
Arranged by Dan Coates

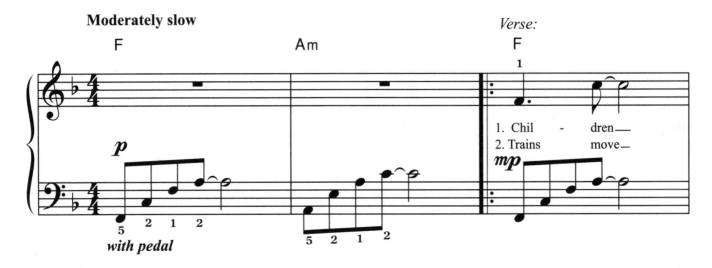

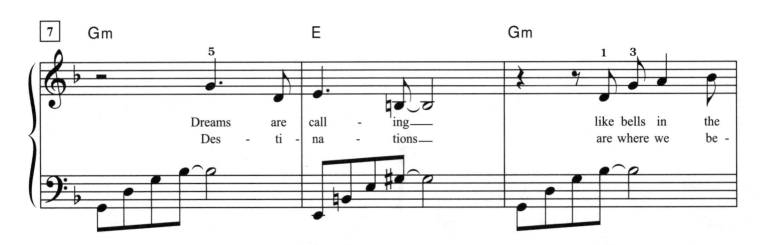

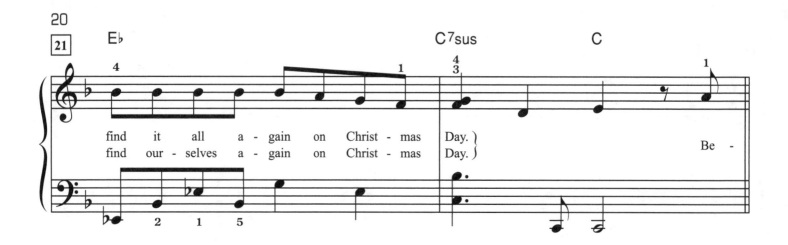

21 | E♭ | C7sus | C

find it all a - gain on Christ - mas Day.
find our - selves a - gain on Christ - mas Day.

Be -

Chorus:

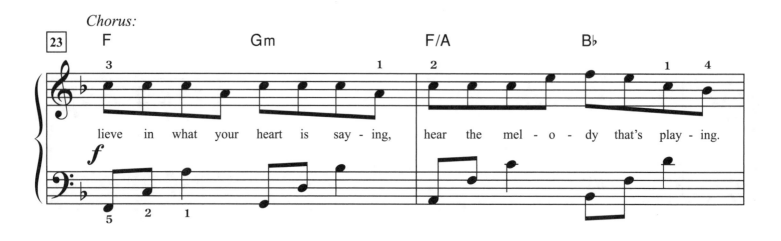

23 | F | Gm | F/A | B♭

lieve in what your heart is say - ing, hear the mel - o - dy that's play - ing.

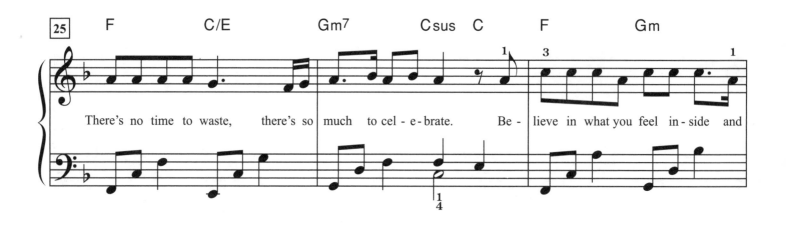

25 | F | C/E | Gm7 | Csus | C | F | Gm

There's no time to waste, there's so much to cel - e - brate. Be - lieve in what you feel in - side and

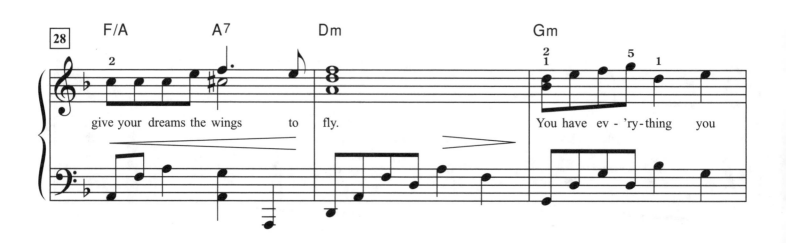

28 | F/A | A7 | Dm | Gm

give your dreams the wings to fly. You have ev - 'ry - thing you

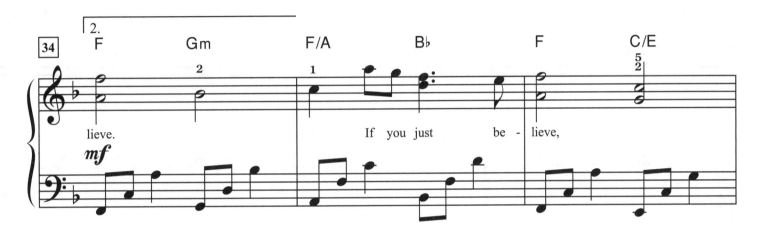

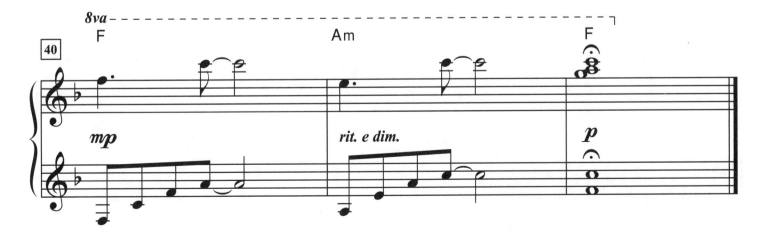

BOULEVARD OF BROKEN DREAMS

This hit single from Green Day's 2004 album, *American Idiot*, won a Grammy for Record of the Year and garnered six MTV Video Music awards. As an album, *American Idiot* catapulted Green Day into mainstream success and earned the band a Grammy for Best Rock Album in 2005.

Words by Billie Joe Music by Green Day
Arranged by Dan Coates

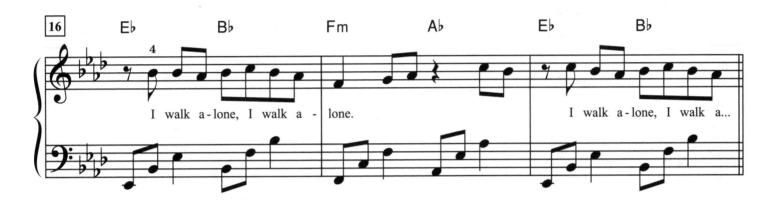

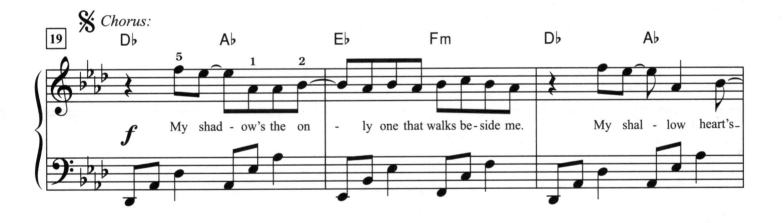

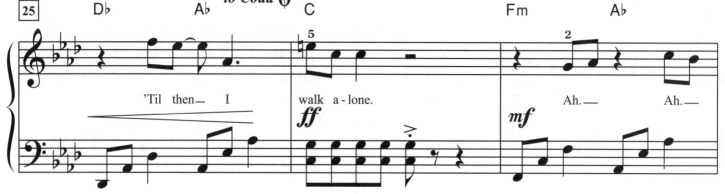

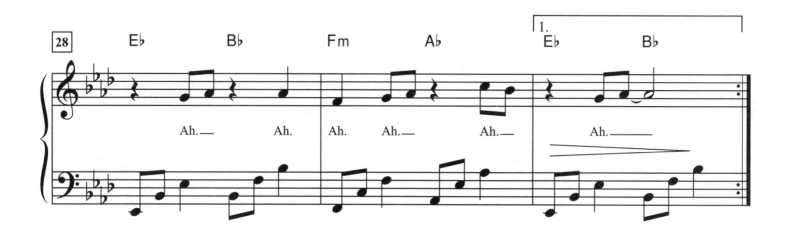

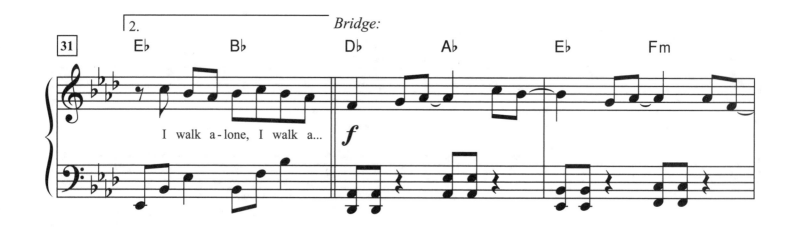

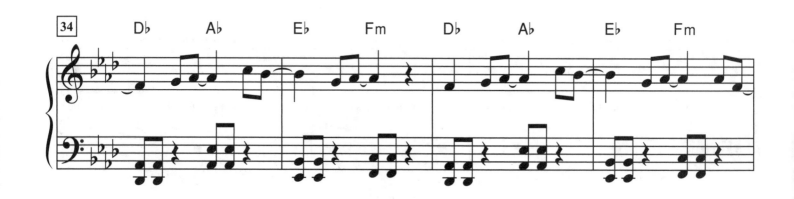

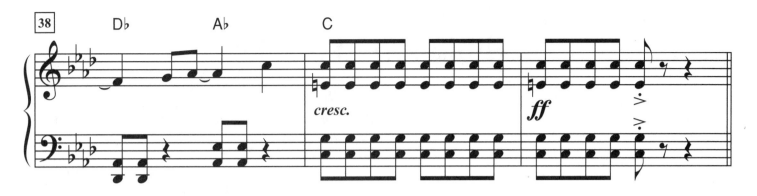

38 D♭ A♭ C

cresc. *ff*

Verse:

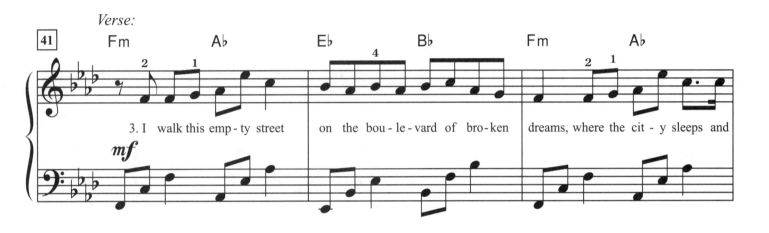

41 Fm A♭ Eb B♭ Fm A♭

3. I walk this emp - ty street on the bou - le - vard of bro - ken dreams, where the cit - y sleeps and

mf

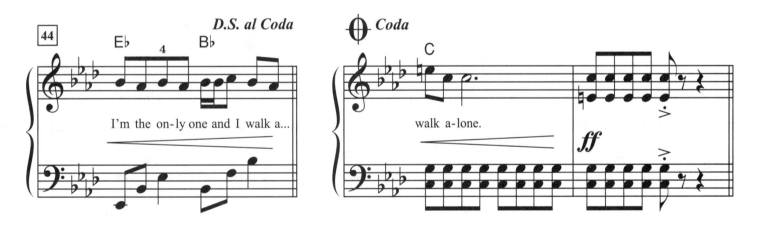

44 E♭ B♭ **D.S. al Coda** **Coda** C

I'm the on - ly one and I walk a... walk a - lone.

ff

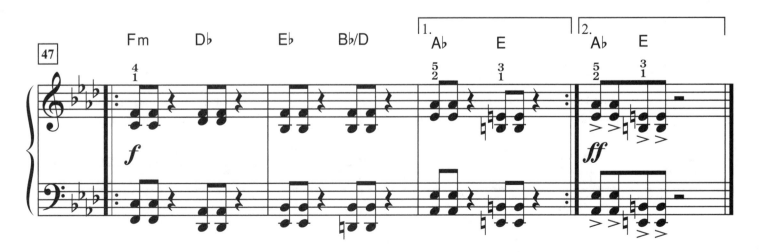

47 Fm D♭ E♭ B♭/D 1. A♭ E 2. A♭ E

f *ff*

BRING ME TO LIFE

This is the first single from Evanescence's 2003 debut album *Fallen.* The album went multi-platinum, garnered two Grammy awards, and "Bring Me to Life" was a worldwide hit, topping both the modern and mainstream rock charts. The co-founders of Evanescence, Amy Lee and Ben Moody, have parted ways but both have continued dynamic careers in the music industry. Moody helped pen Kelly Clarkson's popular hit "Because of You" (page 4).

Words and Music by
Ben Moody, Amy Lee, and David Hodges
Arranged by Dan Coates

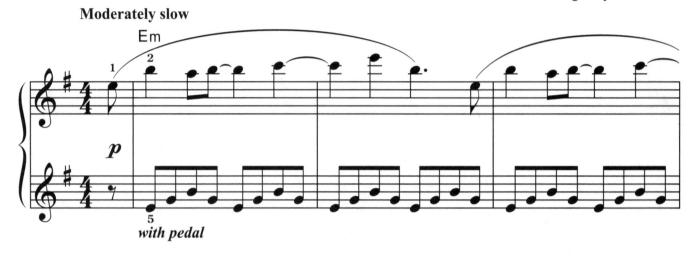

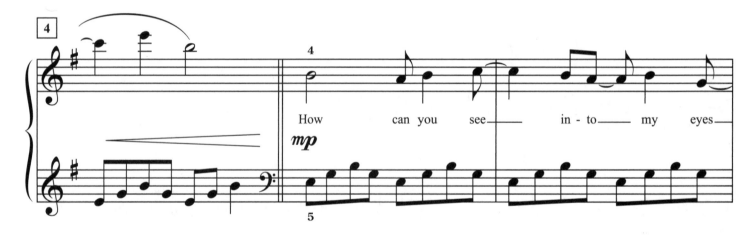

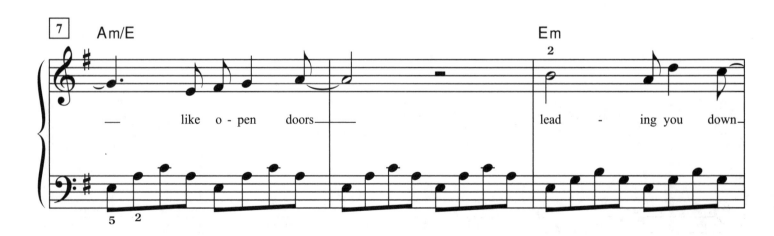

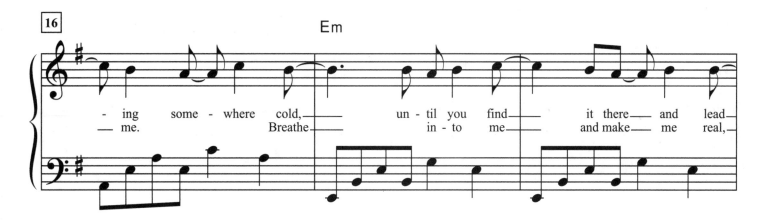

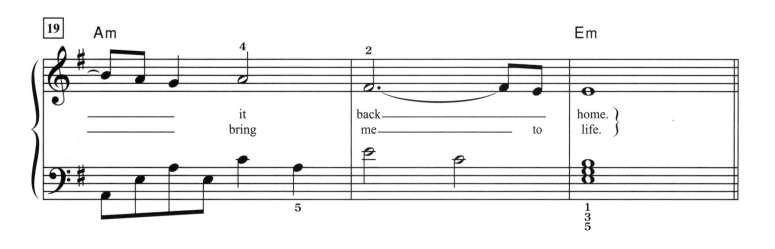

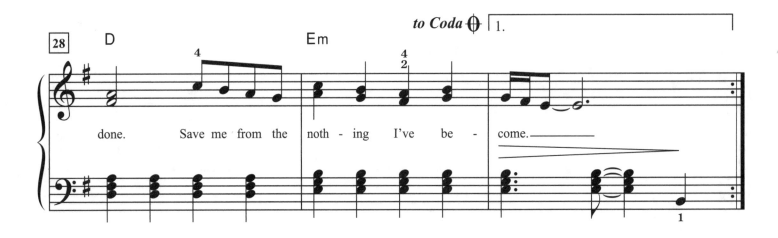

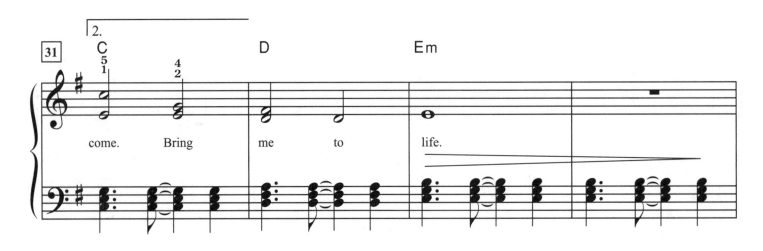

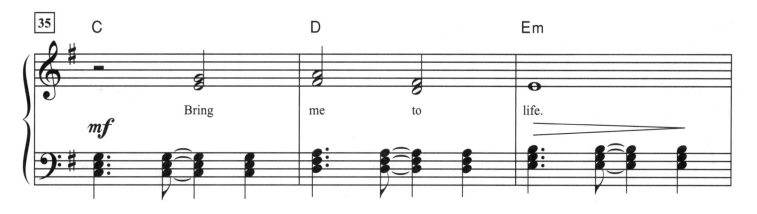

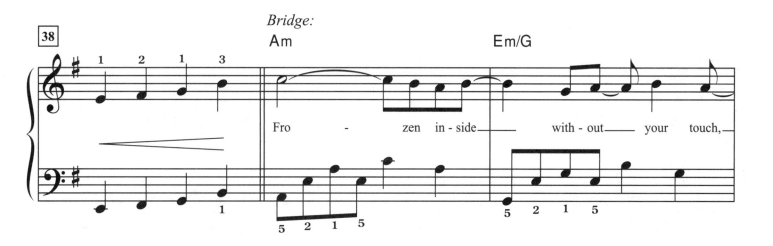

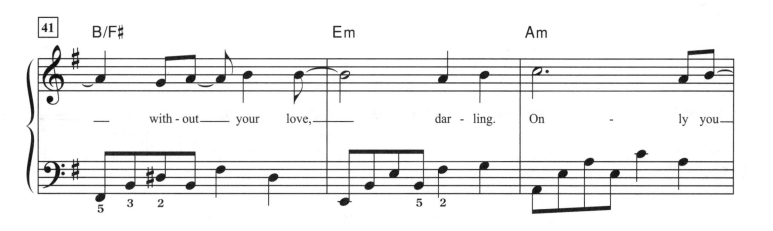

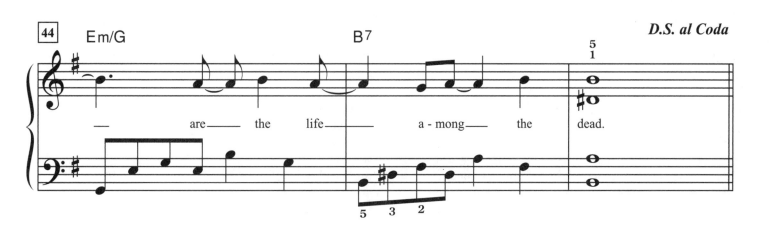

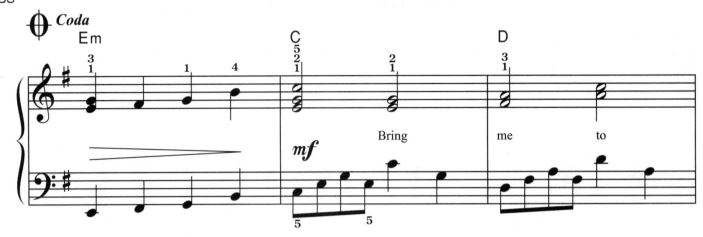

Verse 3:
All this time I can't believe I couldn't see.
Kept in the dark, but you were there in front of me.
I've been sleeping a thousand years, it seems.
Got to open my eyes to everything.
Without a thought, without a voice, without a soul.
Don't let me die here.
There must be something more.
Bring me to life.
(To Chorus:)

CALIFORNIA

The Fox television show *The O.C.* aired from 2003 to 2007 and focused on the drama-filled lives of teenagers in California's ritzy Orange County. The theme song was written and performed by Phantom Planet and musically quotes the Al Jolson song "California, Here I Come." Phantom Planet's drummer was Jason Schwartzman, who is known for his acting roles in movies such as *Rushmore*, *I Heart Huckabees*, and *Marie Antoinette*, to name a few.

Words and Music by Al Jolson, B.G. Desylva,
Joseph Meyer, Jason Schwartzman and Alex Greenwald
Arranged by Dan Coates

CRY ME A RIVER

Justified (released November 2002) marked Justin Timberlake's first solo album after a successful career with the boy band N*SYNC. The single "Cry Me a River," inspired by his break-up from girlfriend Britney Spears, won Timberlake a Grammy for Best Male Pop Vocal Performance in 2004.

Words and Music by
Justin Timberlake, Timothy Z. Mosley and Scott Storch
Arranged by Dan Coates

With a moderate, steady beat

Verse 2:
I know that they say that some things are better left unsaid.
But it wasn't like you only talked to him and you know it.
All of these things people told me keep messin' with my head.
You should've picked honestly, then you may not have blown it.
You don't have to say what you did.
I already know, I found out from him.
Now there's just no chance for you and me,
There'll never be,
And don't it make you sad?
(To Chorus:)

DANCE WITH MY FATHER

Dance with My Father was Luther Vandross' final studio album before his untimely death in 2005. The eponymous single, dedicated to Vandross' late father, won a 2004 Grammy for Best Male R & B Vocal Performance as well as Song of the Year. Despite Vandross' multitude of studio albums and mainstream success, *Dance with My Father* was the only one to achieve success on the Billboard charts.

Words and Music by
Richard Marx and Luther Vandross
Arranged by Dan Coates

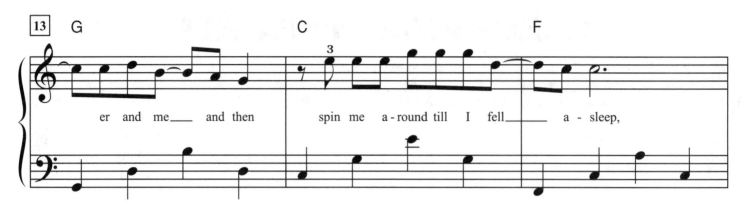

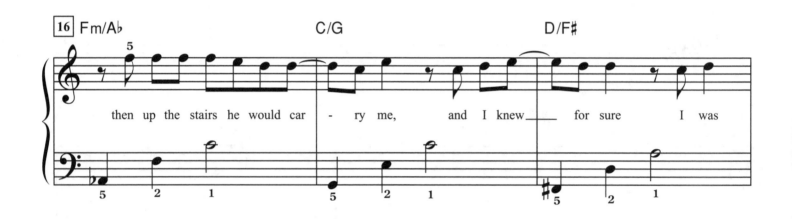

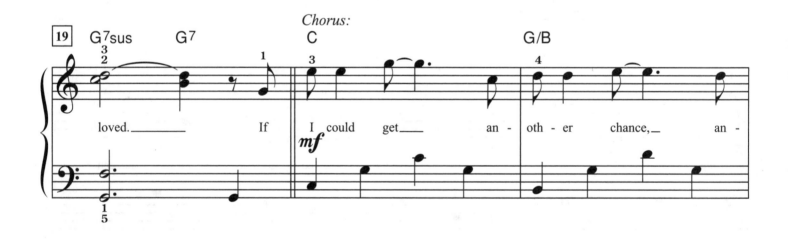

er, ev-er end. How I'd love, love, love to dance with my fa-ther a-

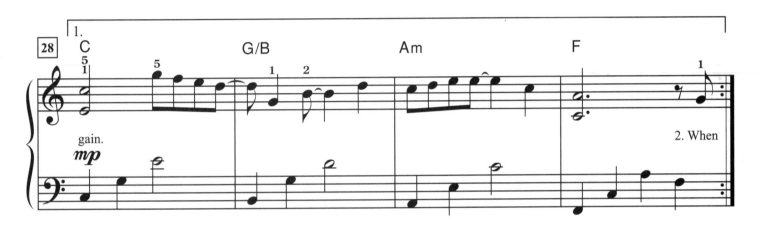

gain.

2. When

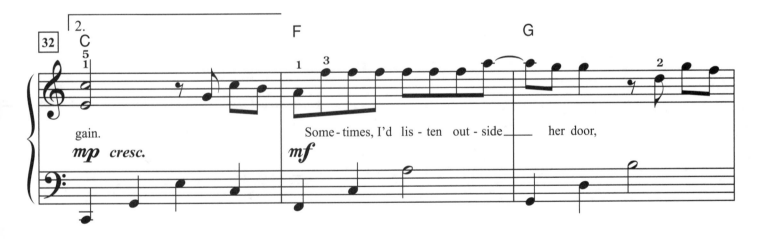

gain.

Some-times, I'd lis-ten out-side her door,

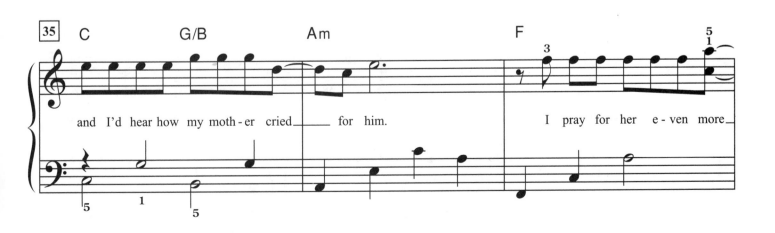

and I'd hear how my moth-er cried for him.

I pray for her e-ven more

42

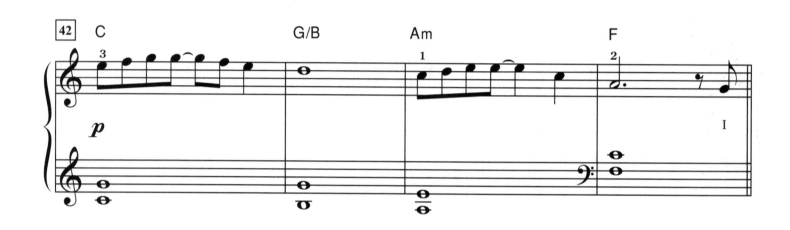

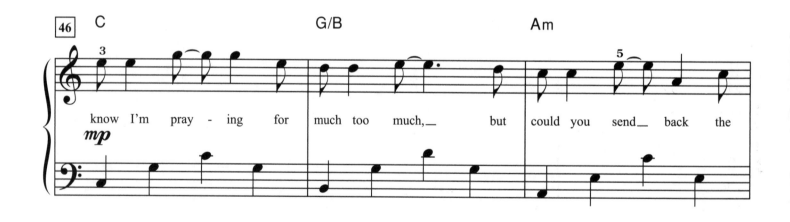

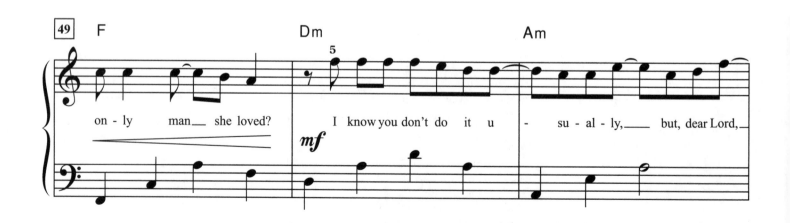

she's dy - ing to dance with my fa - ther a - gain.

Ev - 'ry night I fall a - sleep, and this is all I ev - er dream.

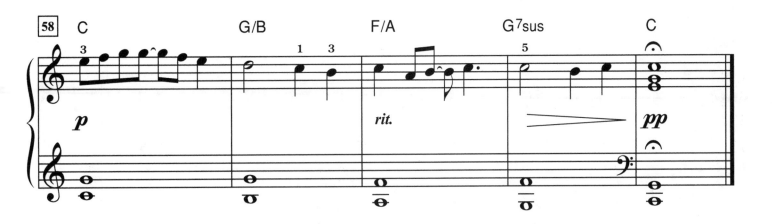

Verse 2:
When I and my mother would disagree,
To get my way, I would run from her to him.
He'd make me laugh just to comfort me,
Then finally make me do just what my mama said.
Later that night, when I was asleep,
He'd left a dollar under my sheet.
Never dreamed that would be gone from me.

Chorus 2:
If I could steal one final glance,
One final step,
One final dance with him,
I'd play a song that would never, ever end.
'Cause I'd love, love, love
To dance with my father again.

DON'T STOP THE MUSIC

This Grammy-nominated dance hit dominated the airwaves during the summer of 2007. Just two years earlier, Rihanna (Robyn Rihanna Fenty) burst onto the music scene with her popular "Pon de Replay." "Don't Stop the Music" appeared on her third album, *Good Girl Gone Bad*, which was nominated for nine Grammy awards. Another hit from the album, "Umbrella," can be found on page 131.

Words and Music by Michael Jackson, Mikkel Storleer Eriksen,
Tor Erik Hermansen and Frankie Storm
Arranged by Dan Coates

Moderately fast, with a heavy dance beat

DARK KNIGHT OVERTURE
(FROM "THE DARK KNIGHT")

Hans Zimmer and James Newton Howard, who collaborated on the 2005 score for *Batman Begins*, composed the music for the 2008 film *The Dark Knight*, which won the 2009 Grammy for Best Score Soundtrack Album for a Motion Picture. Both composers are powerhouses in the world of film scoring. Zimmer's credits include *Pirates of the Caribbean*, *Gladiator*, and *The Da Vinci Code*, to name a few. Howard's output includes *Pretty Woman*, *The Fugitive*, and *The Sixth Sense*.

Composed by Hans Zimmer and James Newton Howard
Arranged by Dan Coates

FALLING SLOWLY
(FROM "ONCE")

The soundtrack for the 2007 independent film *Once* took the Grammy and Academy awards by storm with nominations for Best Original Song and Soundtrack. "Falling Slowly" won the Academy award for Best Original Song and was performed live at the ceremony by co-stars Glen Hansard and Markéta Irglová. In the movie, they played struggling musicians who cross paths at a crucial time in their lives.

Words and Music by
Glen Hansard and Marketa Irglova
Arranged by Dan Coates

Slowly, with expression

Verse:

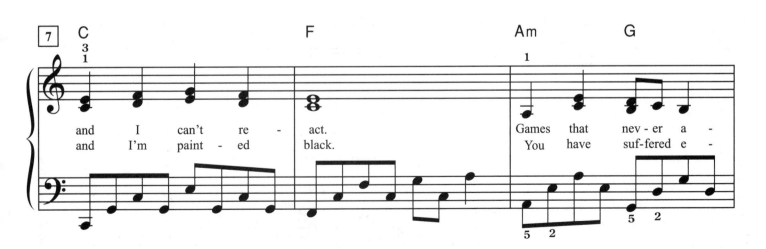

Chorus:

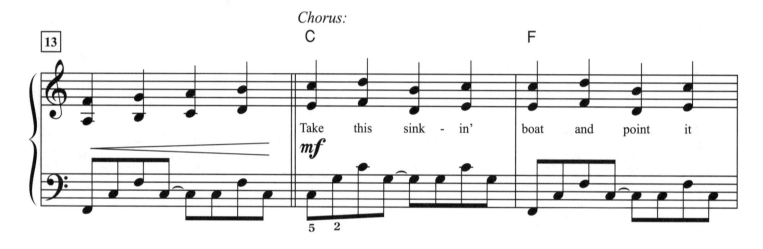

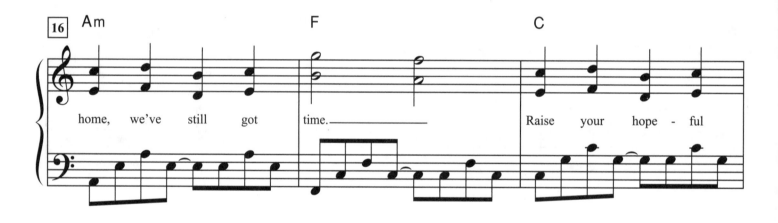

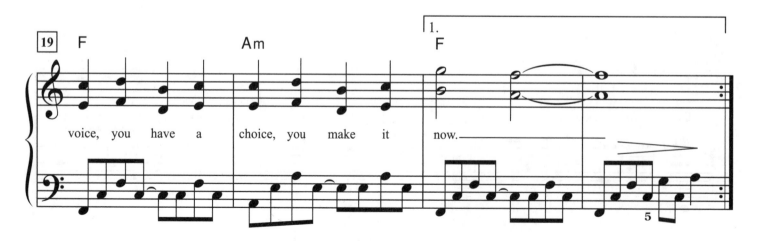

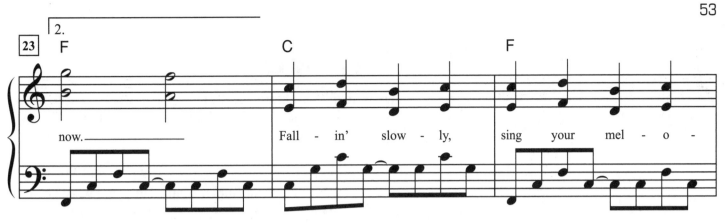

now.＿＿＿＿ Fall - in' slow - ly, sing your mel - o -

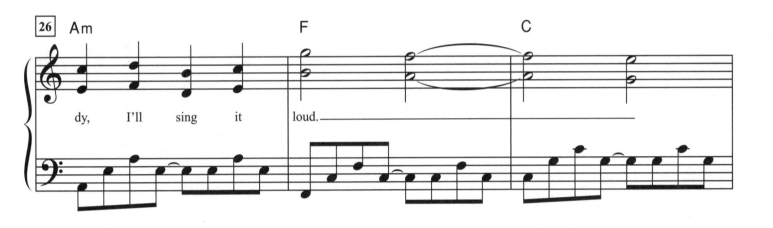

dy, I'll sing it loud.＿＿＿＿＿＿＿＿

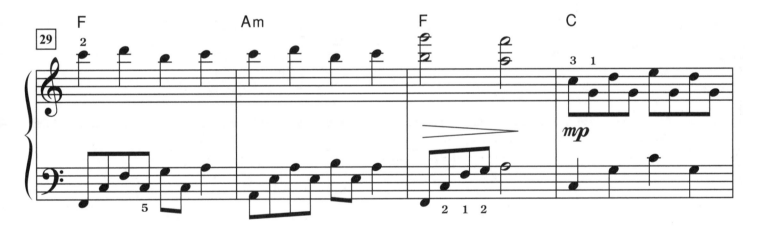

dim. p rit. e dim. pp

EVERYTHING

Much like his 2005 hit "Home" (page 80), "Everything" ventured into the adult contemporary market, a rarity for Michael Bublé who is known for his big band and jazz style. "Everything" (from the album *Call Me Irresponsible*) was nominated for a Grammy award in 2007. The same year, the album reached No. 1 on the Billboard 200 chart.

Words and Music by
Michael Bublé, Alan Chang and Amy Foster
Arranged by Dan Coates

Moderately, with a steady beat

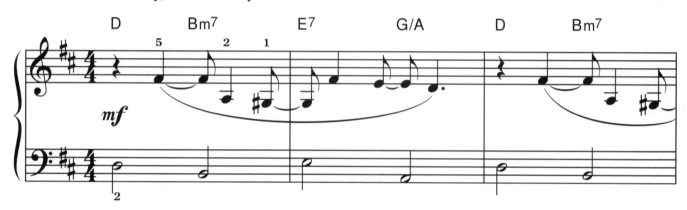

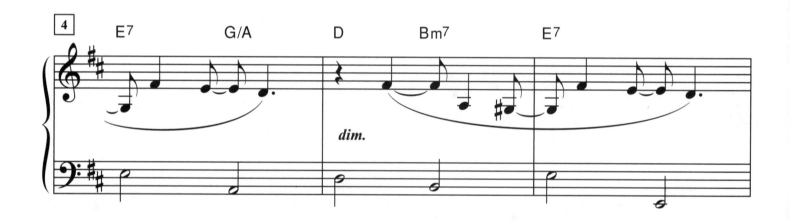

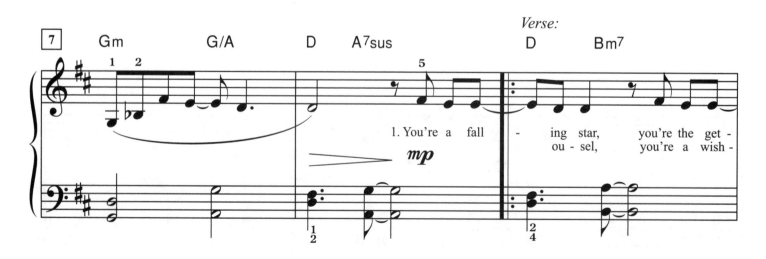

THE GAME OF LOVE

Carlos Santana's 2002 album, *Shaman*, was chock-full of collaborations with a wide range of popular and classical musicians. "The Game of Love" featured vocalist Michelle Branch who had just gained recognition a year earlier for her hit "Everywhere." "The Game of Love" won the 2003 Grammy for Best Pop Collaboration with Vocals and had a solid run on the Billboard charts.

Words and Music by Gregg Alexander and Rick Nowells
Arranged by Dan Coates

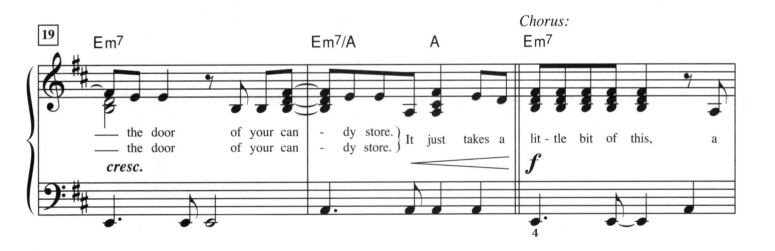

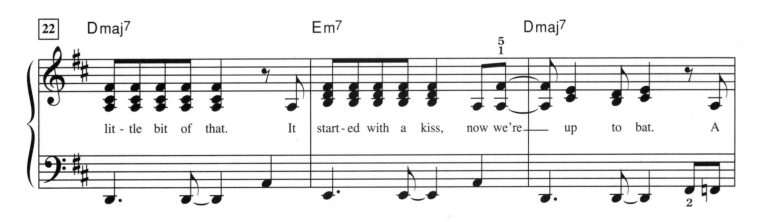

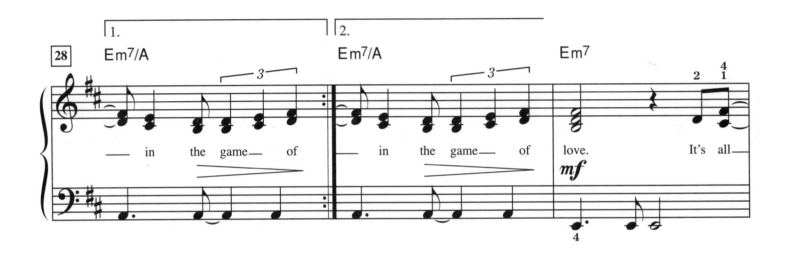

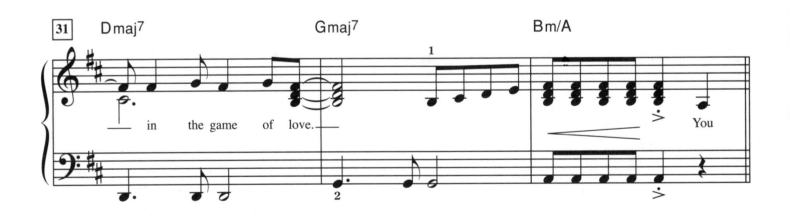

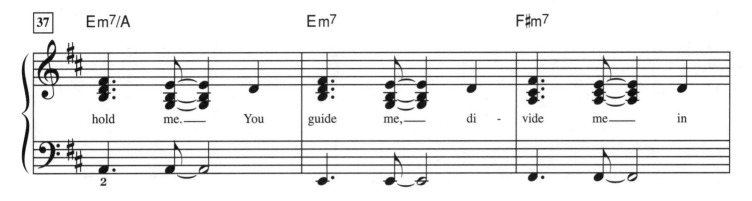

hold me.___ You guide me,___ di - vide me___ in

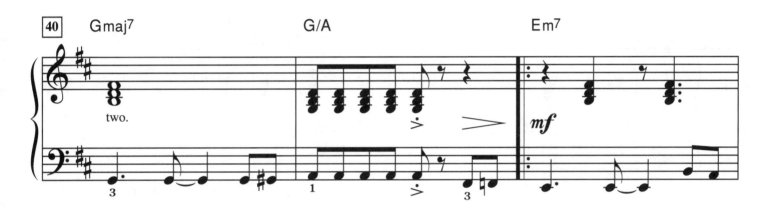

two.

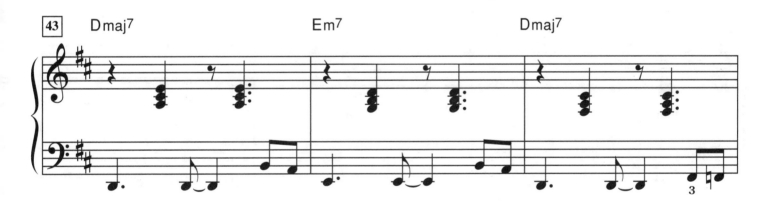

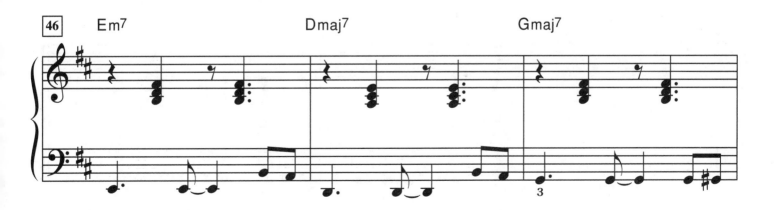

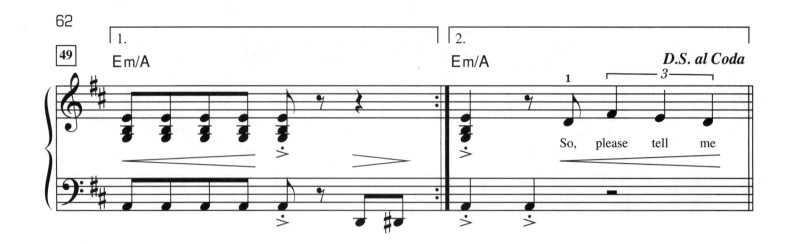

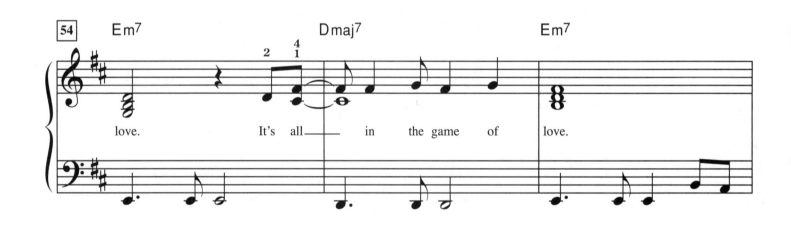

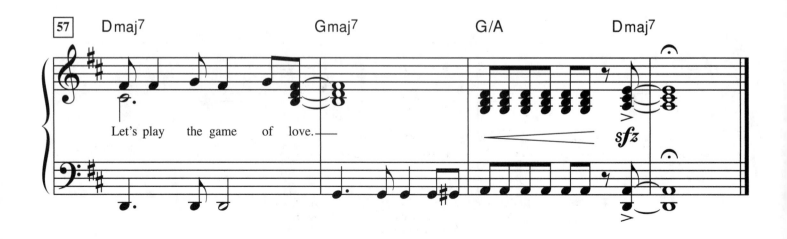

HEY THERE DELILAH

While "Hey There Delilah" was the third single from Plain White T's 2005 album *All That We Needed*, it was their first huge hit and reached No. 1 on the Billboard Hot 100 in July of 2007. Their follow-up album, *Every Second Counts*, offered a bonus track of "Hey There Delilah" with a string section.

Words and Music by Tom Higgenson
Arranged by Dan Coates

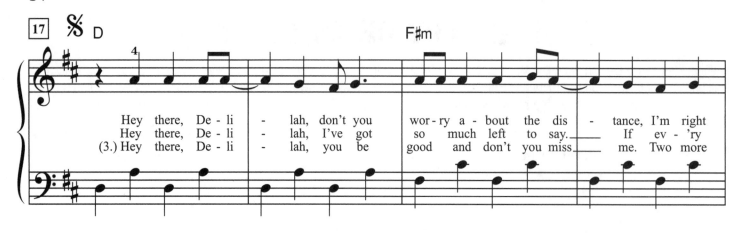

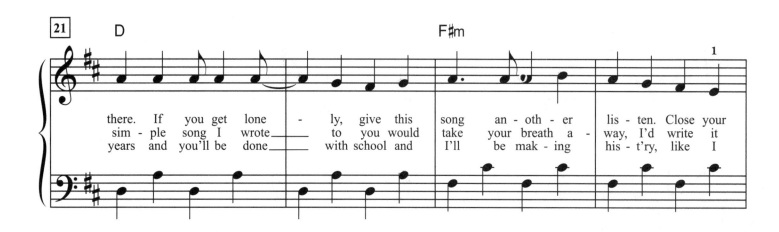

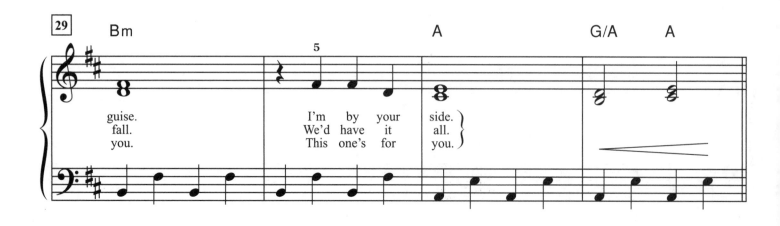

HEDWIG'S THEME
(FROM "HARRY POTTER AND THE SORCERER'S STONE")

British author J. K. Rowling's *Harry Potter* fantasy novels have sold over 400 million copies worldwide, due in part to their transformation into series of blockbuster movies. John Williams composed "Hedwig's Theme" for *Harry Potter and the Sorcerer's Stone*, the first installment in the series, and the theme has been used in each film since.

By **JOHN WILLIAMS**
Arranged by Dan Coates

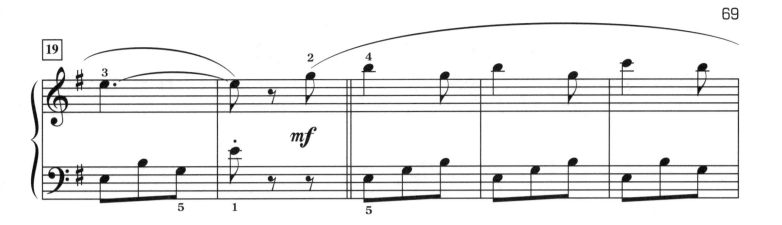

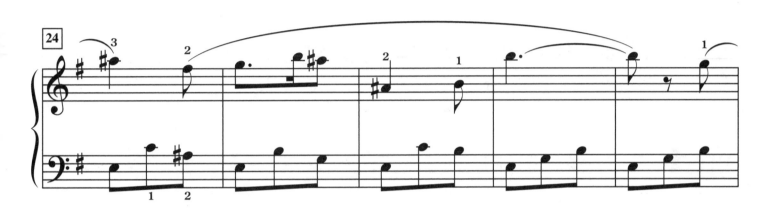

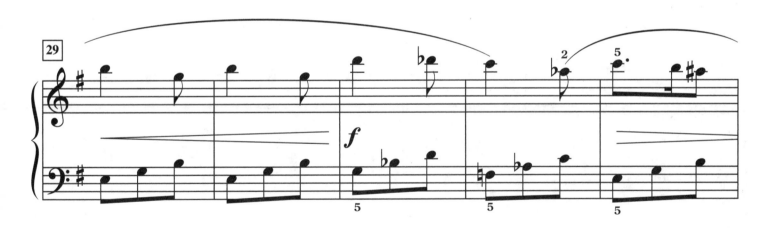

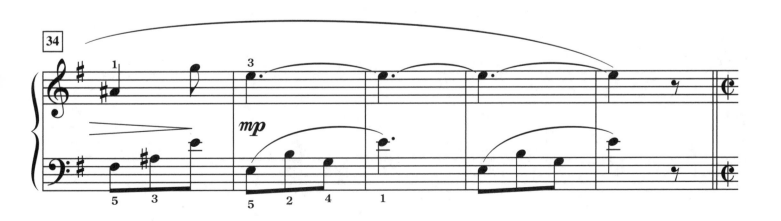

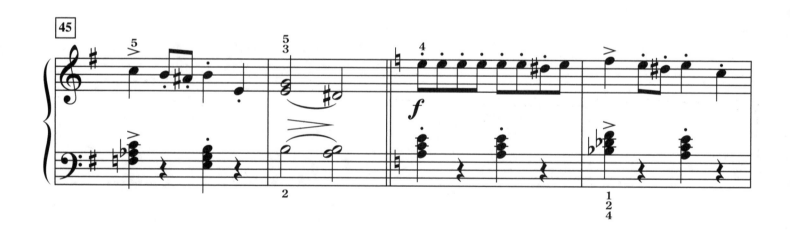

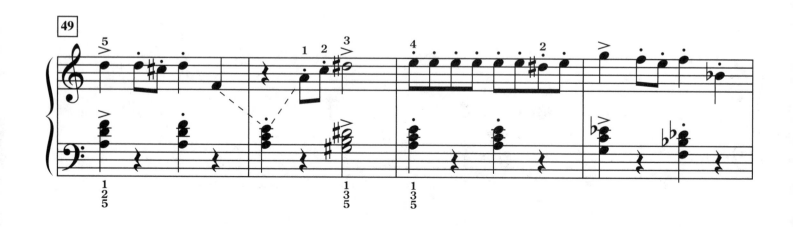

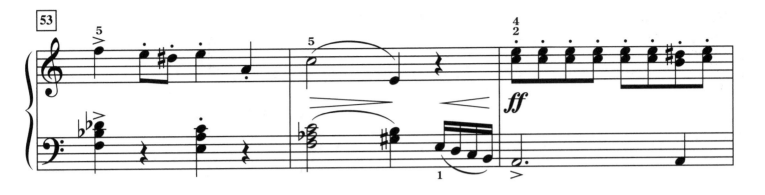

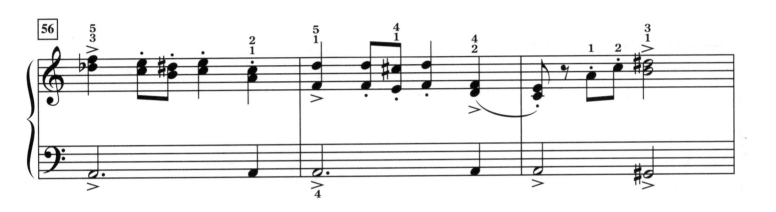

HIGH

James Blunt's single "High" garnered success following his 2005 chart-topper "You're Beautiful." Included on his first album *Back to Bedlam*, "High" was inspired when Blunt watched a beautiful sunrise.

Words and Music by Ricky Ross and James Blunt
Arranged by Dan Coates

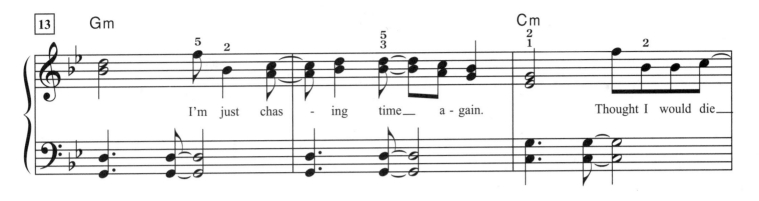

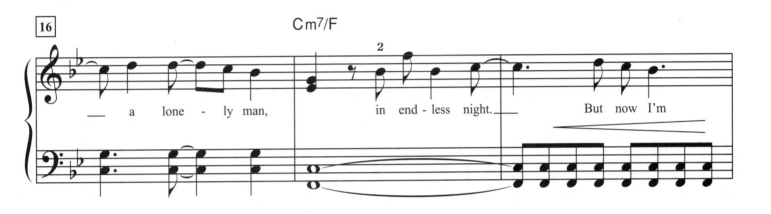

Chorus:

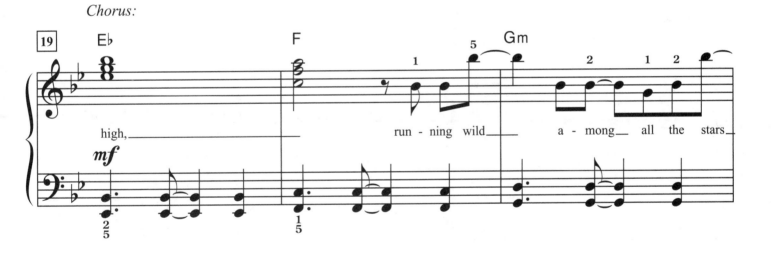

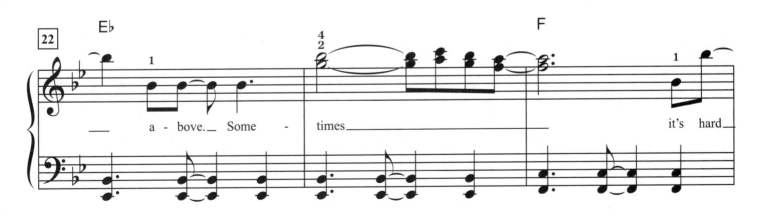

to be - lieve you re - mem - ber me. _ - ber me. _

Bridge:

Will you be my shoul - der when I'm grey and old - er? Prom - ise me to - mor - row

Chorus:

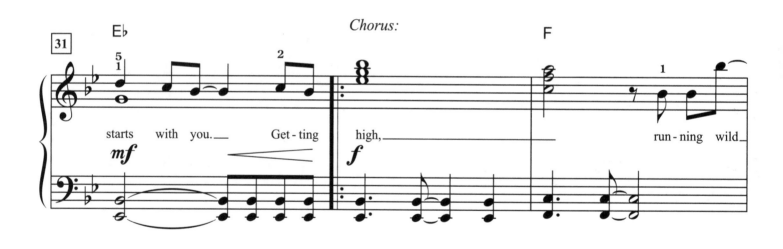

starts with you. _ Get - ting high, _ run - ning wild _

_ a - mong _ all the stars _ a - bove. _ Some - times _

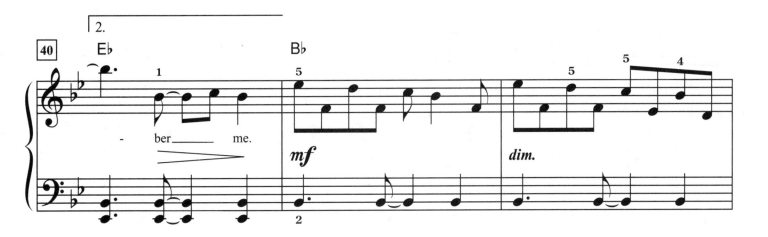

it's hard___ to be-lieve you re-mem - ber me.___

-ber___ me.

mf

dim.

mp

rit. e dim.

p

Verse 2:
Beautiful dawn,
Melt with the stars again.
Do you remember
The day when my journey began?
Will you remember
The end of time?
Beautiful dawn,
You're just blowing my mind again.
Thought I was born
To endless night,
Until you shine.
(To Chorus:)

HOW LUCKY YOU ARE
(FROM "SEUSSICAL")

Penned by the Tony award-winning duo of Stephen Flaherty (composer) and Lynn Ahrens (lyricist), *Seussical* debuted on Broadway in 2000. The musical weaves a variety of characters and plotlines from the stories of Dr. Seuss. Flaherty and Ahrens are also known for their shows *Ragtime*, *Once on This Island*, and *A Man of No Importance*, to name a few.

Lyrics by Lynn Ahrens
Music by Stephen Flaherty
Arranged by Dan Coates

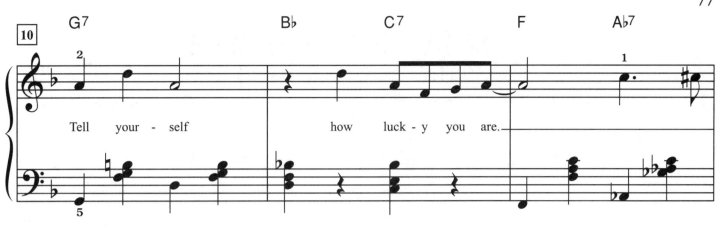

Tell your - self how luck - y you are.

When your life's go - ing wrong,— when the fates are un - kind,— when you're

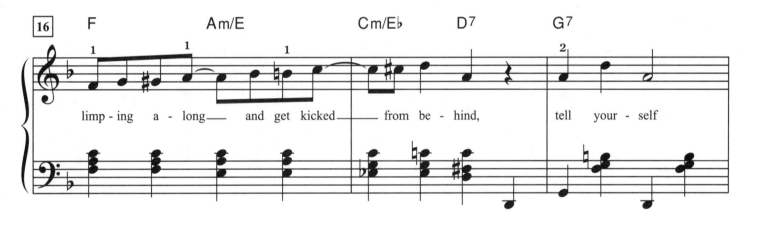

limp - ing a - long— and get kicked— from be - hind, tell your - self

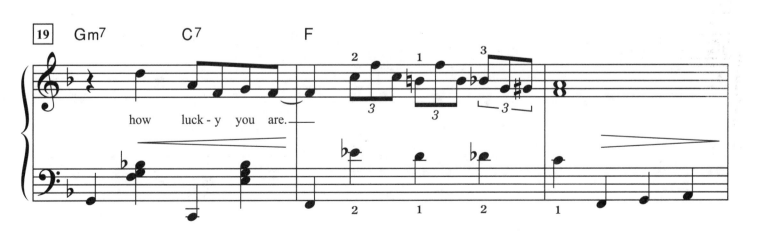

how luck - y you are.

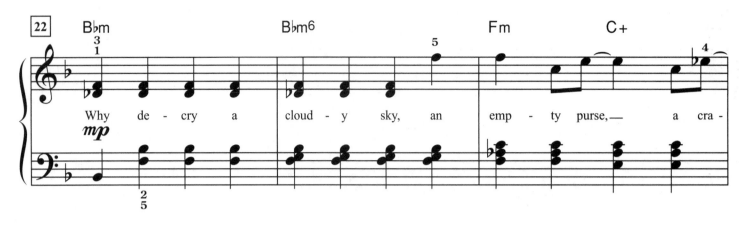

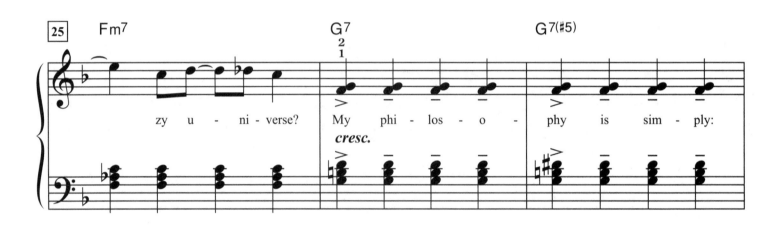

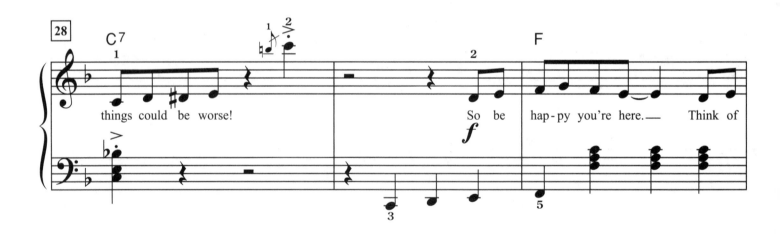

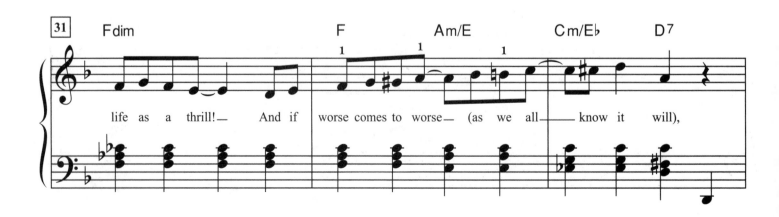

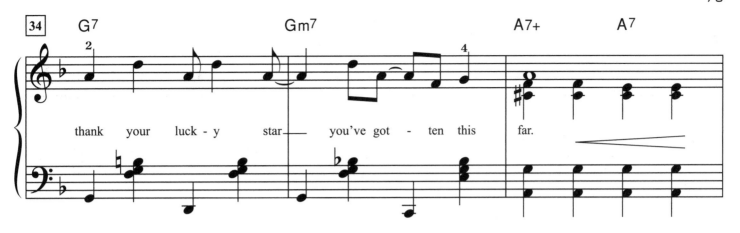

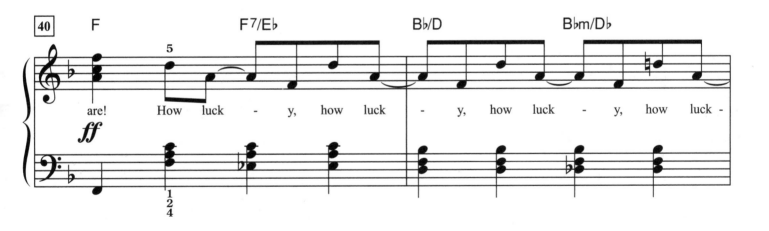

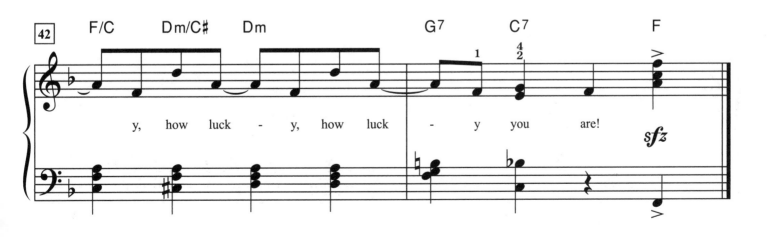

HOME

Featured on Michael Bublé's second album, *It's Time* (2005), "Home" was written by Bublé, Alan Chang (his music director), and Amy Foster (producer David Foster's daughter). The song topped the charts in both Canada and the U. S., crossing over from the adult contemporary to the pop charts. In 2008, country artist Blake Shelton's version of "Home" reached the top of the Billboard Hot Country Songs chart.

Words and Music by
Michael Bublé, Alan Chang and Amy Foster
Arranged by Dan Coates

IN DREAMS
(FROM "THE LORD OF THE RINGS: THE FELLOWSHIP OF THE RING")

The Lord of the Rings: The Fellowship of the Ring is one of the highest grossing movies of all time. Since its 2001 release, two other films based on the J. R. R. Tolkien books have been made under the direction of Peter Jackson. The lyricist of "In Dreams," Fran Walsh, is also the life and business partner of Jackson.

Words and Music by Fran Walsh and Howard Shore
Arranged by Dan Coates

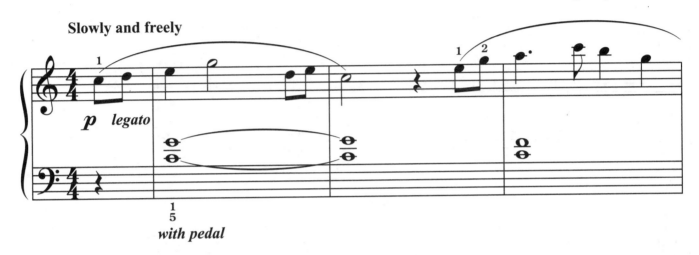

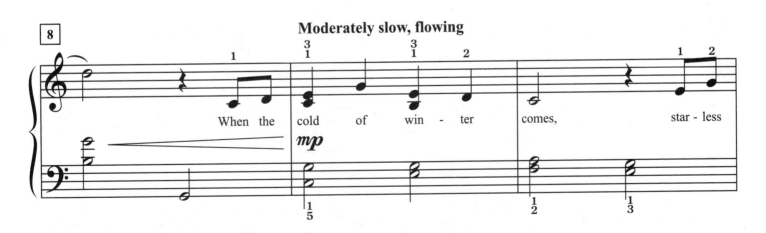

I KISSED A GIRL

Katy Perry burst onto the pop scene with a bang in the summer of 2008 with this rock anthem. "I Kissed a Girl" was the first single from Perry's album *One of the Boys* and landed in the number one spot on the Billboard Hot 100 chart. Perry performed the song at the Grammy Awards where she was nominated for Best Female Pop Vocal Performance.

Words and Music by Katy Perry,
Lukasz Gottwald, Max Martin and Cathy Dennis
Arranged by Dan Coates

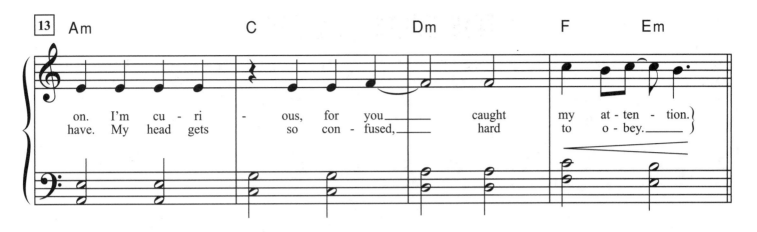

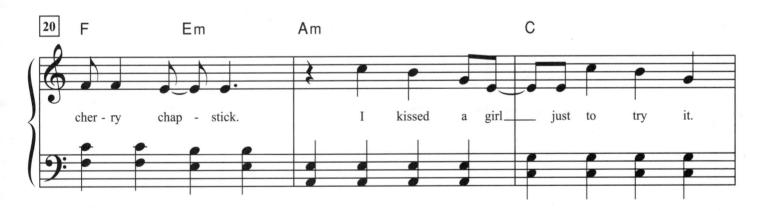

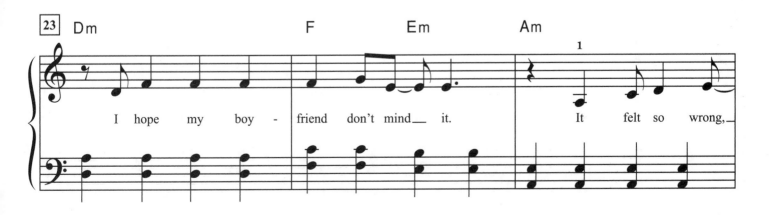

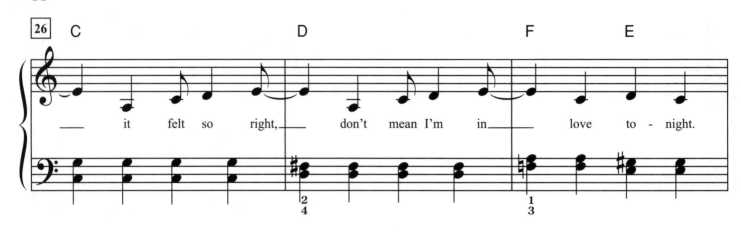

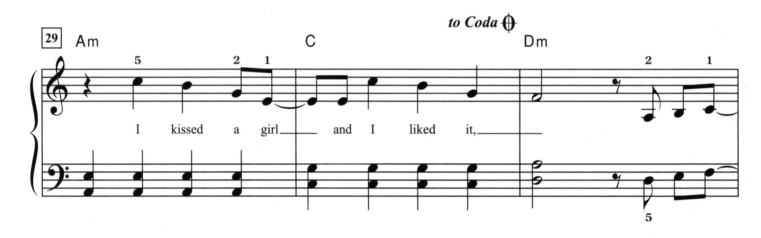

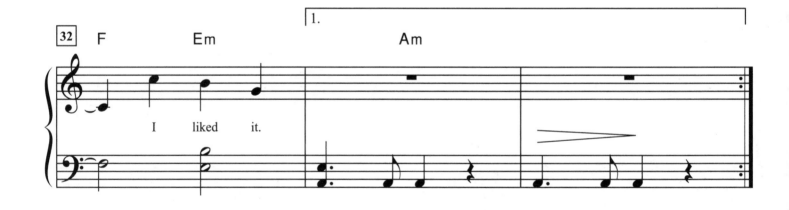

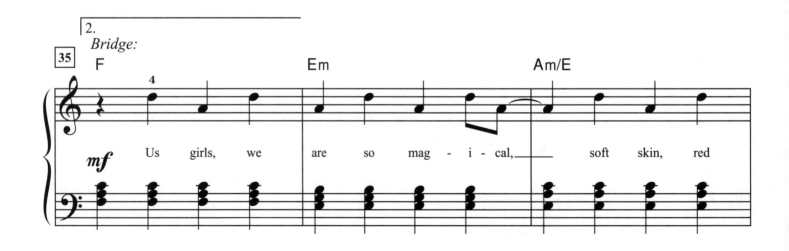

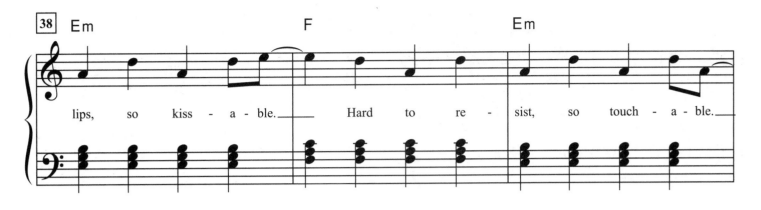

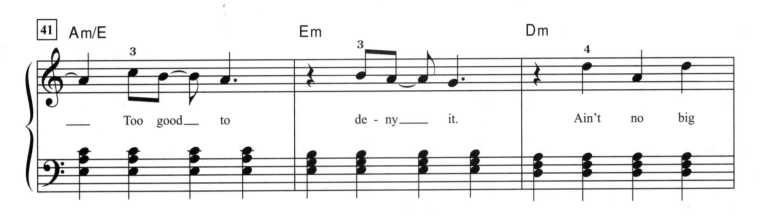

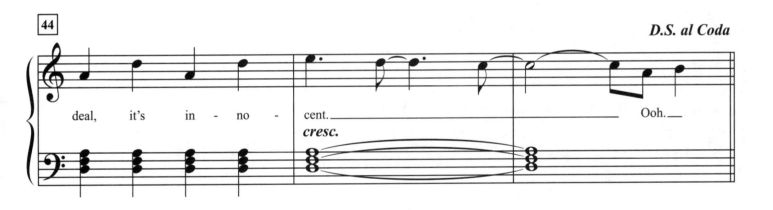

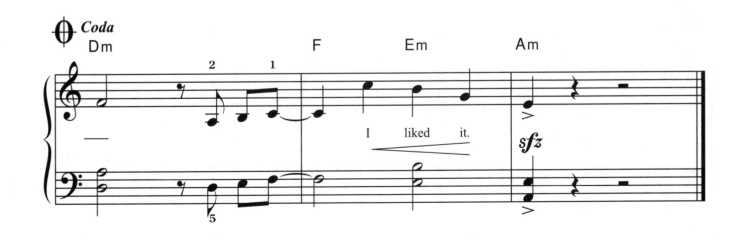

KNOW YOUR ENEMY

Released in the summer of 2009, *21st Century Breakdown* was punk band Green Day's eighth studio album. "Know Your Enemy" was the first single and topped the Billboard charts immediately. The politically charged album echoes many of the sentiments from Green Day's blockbuster album *American Idiot* from 2004.

Lyrics by Billie Joe Music by Green Day
Arranged by Dan Coates

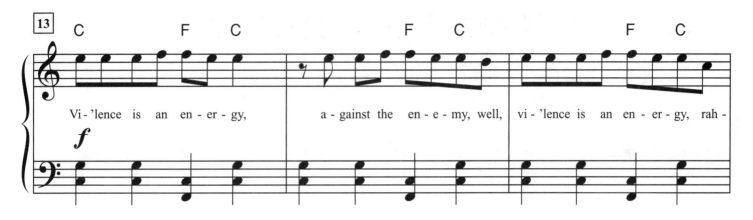

13 C   F   C   F   C   F   C

Vi - 'lence is an en - er - gy,   a - gainst the en - e - my, well,   vi - 'lence is an en - er - gy, rah -

16 G   C   F   C   F   C

eh.   Bring - ing on the fu - ry,   the cho - ir in - fan - try, re -

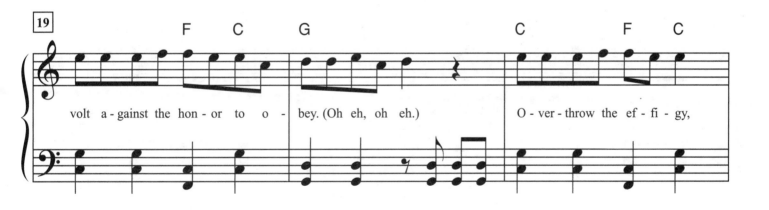

19   F   C   G   C   F   C

volt a - gainst the hon - or to o - bey. (Oh eh, oh eh.)   O - ver - throw the ef - fi - gy,

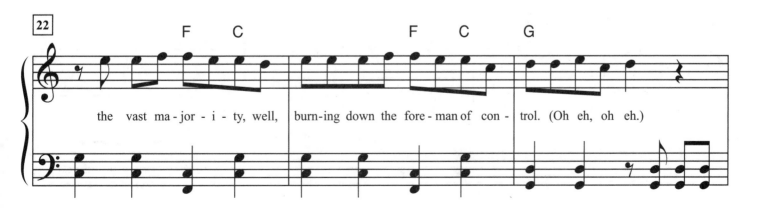

22   F   C   F   C   G

the vast ma - jor - i - ty, well,   burn - ing down the fore - man of con - trol. (Oh eh, oh eh.)

Si - lence is the en - e - my, a - gainst your ur - gen - cy, so ral - ly up the de - mons of your

soul. (Oh eh, oh eh.) Do you know the en - e - my? Do you know your en - e - my? Well,

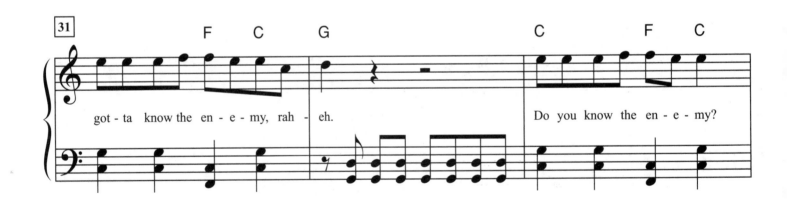

got - ta know the en - e - my, rah - eh. Do you know the en - e - my?

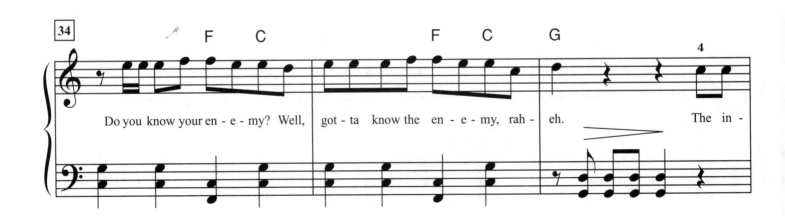

Do you know your en - e - my? Well, got - ta know the en - e - my, rah - eh. The in -

Verse:

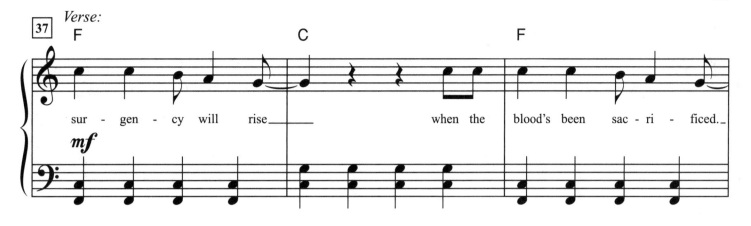

sur - gen - cy will rise_____ when the blood's been sac - ri - ficed._

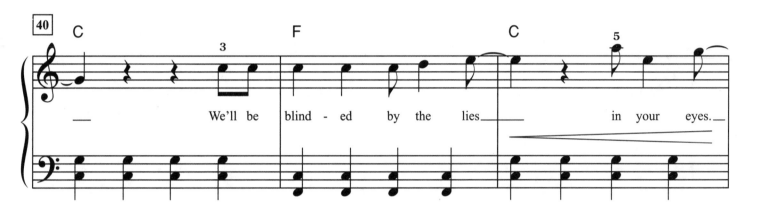

_ We'll be blind - ed by the lies_____ in your eyes._

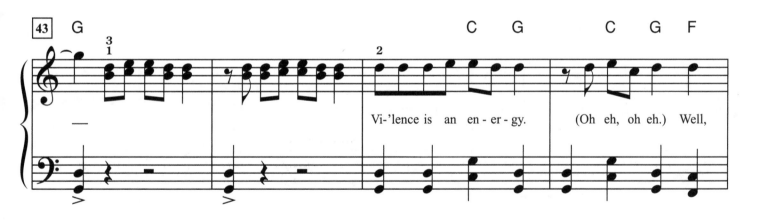

_ Vi - 'lence is an en - er - gy. (Oh eh, oh eh.) Well,

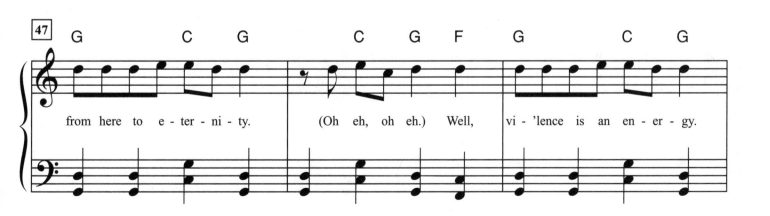

from here to e - ter - ni - ty. (Oh eh, oh eh.) Well, vi - 'lence is an en - er - gy.

D.C. al Coda

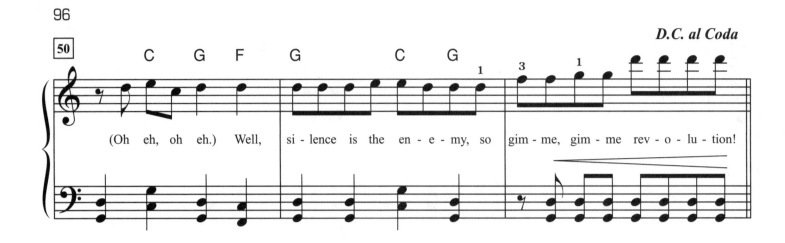

(Oh eh, oh eh.) Well, si - lence is the en - e - my, so gim - me, gim - me rev - o - lu - tion!

Coda

O - ver - throw the ef - fi - gy, the vast ma - jor - i - ty, well, burn - ing down the fore - man of con -

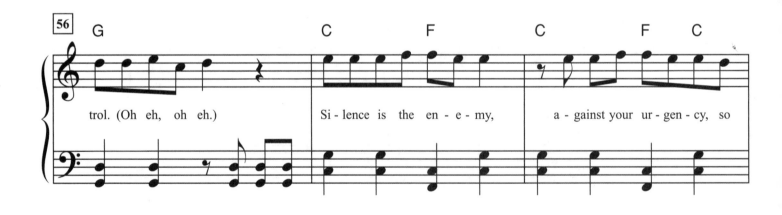

trol. (Oh eh, oh eh.) Si - lence is the en - e - my, a - gainst your ur - gen - cy, so

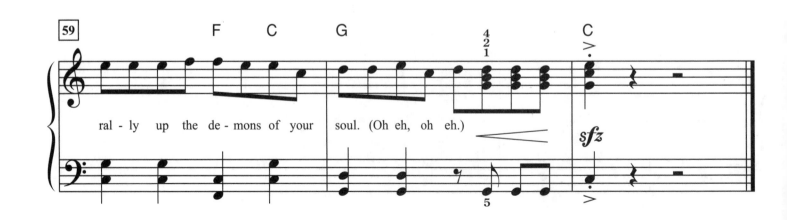

ral - ly up the de - mons of your soul. (Oh eh, oh eh.)

LOST

"Lost" is the second single from Michael Bublé's third studio album, *Call Me Irresponsible.* (The third single, "Everything" is on page 54.) "Lost" reached the No. 2 spot on Billboard's Adult Contemporary charts, as well as strong positioning on the pop charts in Canada and Norway. The song was inspired by Bublé's breakup with his former fiancée, Debbie Timuss.

Words and Music by
Michael Bublé, Alan Chang and Jann Arden
Arranged by Dan Coates

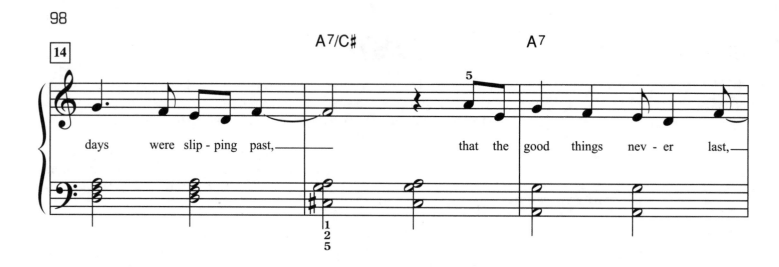

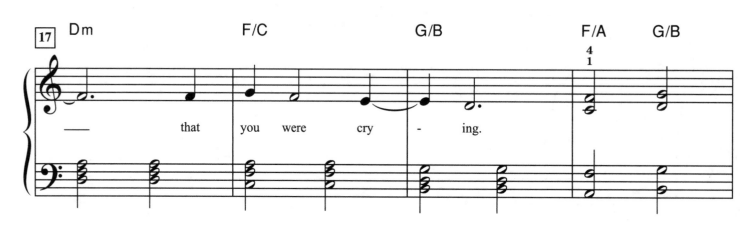

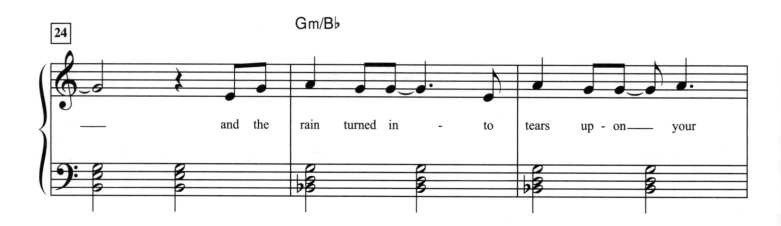

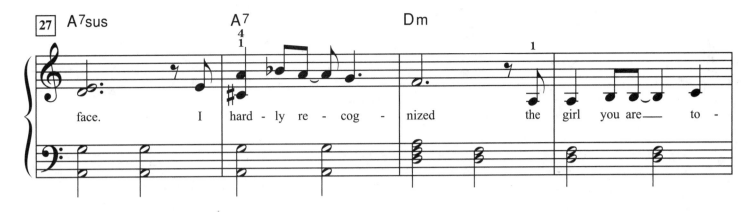

face. I hard - ly re - cog - nized the girl you are — to -

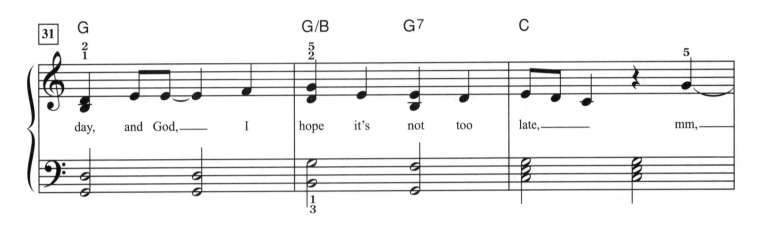

day, and God, — I hope it's not too late, — mm,

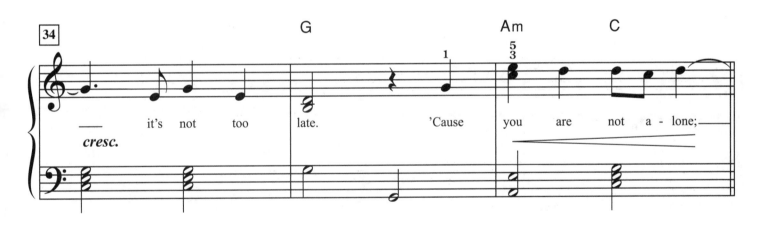

— it's not too late. 'Cause you are not a - lone; —

cresc.

Chorus:

I'm al - ways there — with you. — And we'll get lost to - geth -

f

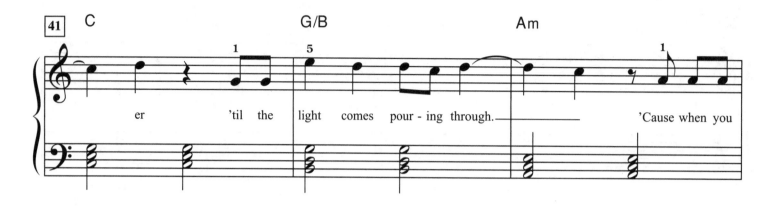

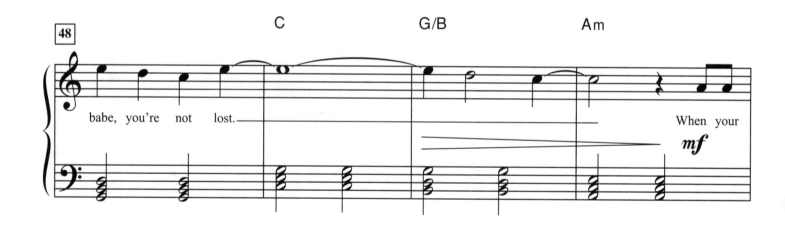

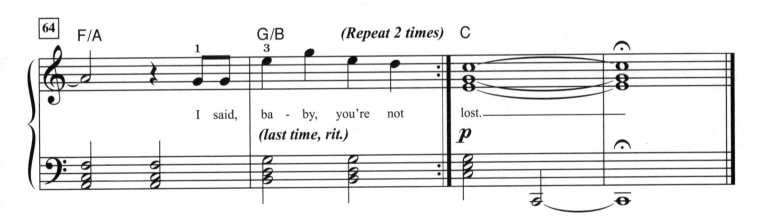

Verse 3:
Life can show no mercy;
It can tear your soul apart.
It can make you feel like you've gone crazy
But you're not.
Though things have seemed to change,
There's one thing that's the same.
In my heart you have remained
And we can fly, fly, fly away.
(To Chorus:)

MY LIFE WOULD SUCK WITHOUT YOU

"My Life Would Suck Without You," from Kelly Clarkson's album *All I Ever Wanted*, reached No. 3 on the Billboard Top 40 chart in 2009. Two of the song's writers, Dr. Luke and Max Martin, also produced and wrote another Clarkson hit, "Since U Been Gone."

Words and Music by
Claude Kelly, Lukasz Gottwald and Max Martin
Arranged by Dan Coates

Said you'd nev - er come ____ back, ____ but here you are ____ a - gain.
Ei - ther way, ____ I found ____ out ____ I'm noth - ing with - out you.

Chorus:

'Cause we be - long ____ to - geth -

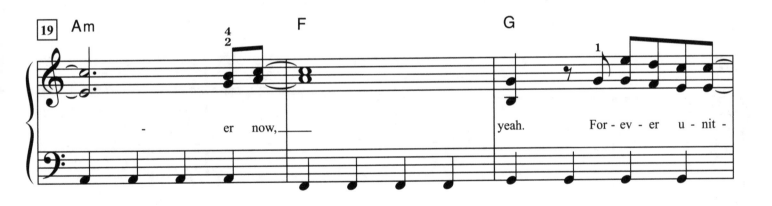

- er now, ____ yeah. For - ev - er u - nit -

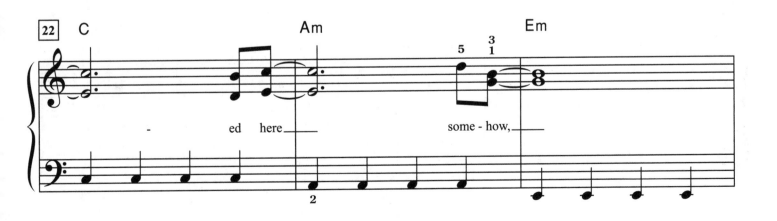

- ed here ____ some - how, ____

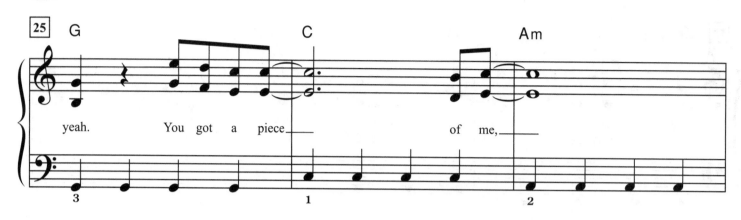

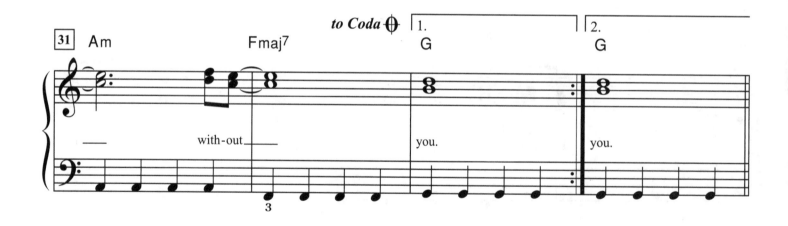

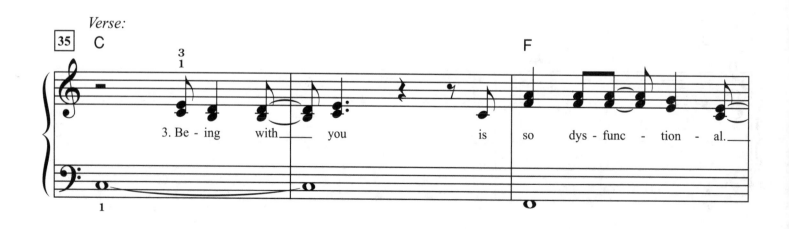

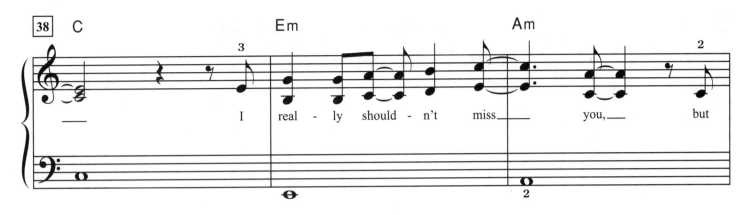

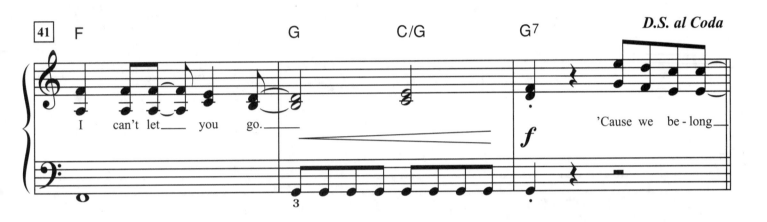

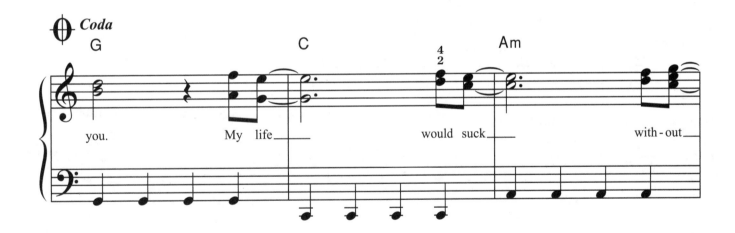

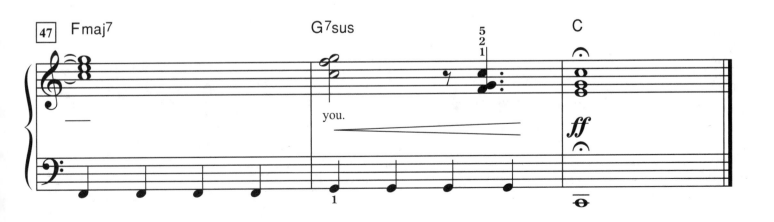

THE NEW GIRL IN TOWN
(FROM "HAIRSPRAY")

The 2007 film adaptation of the musical *Hairpsray* featured an all-star cast including John Travolta, Zac Efron, Michelle Pfeiffer, Christopher Walken, Queen Latifah and many more. "The New Girl in Town" was one of three new songs written for the movie. Composer Marc Shaiman and lyricist Scott Whittman have been professional and life partners since they first met in 1979.

Lyrics by Scott Wittman and Marc Shaiman
Music by Marc Shaiman
Arranged by Dan Coates

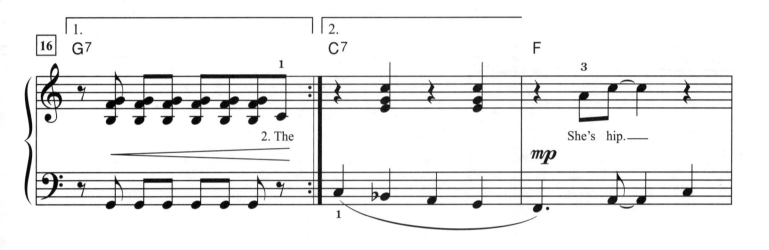

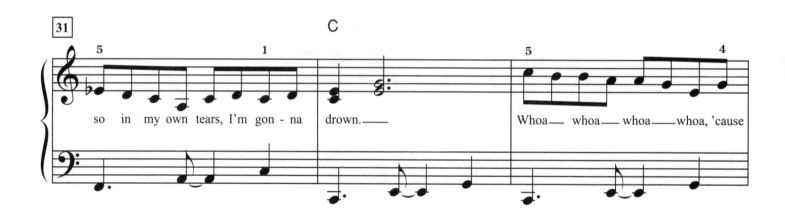

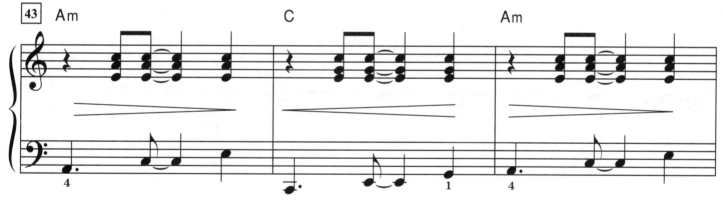

NEW SOUL

Yael Naïm's career was launched when her song "New Soul" was featured in a 2008 Apple Macbook Air ad. The French-Israeli musician became the first Israeli solo artist to have a top ten hit in the U.S.

Words and Music by Yael Naim and David Donatien
Arranged by Dan Coates

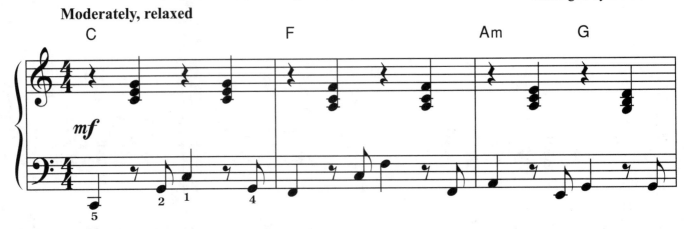

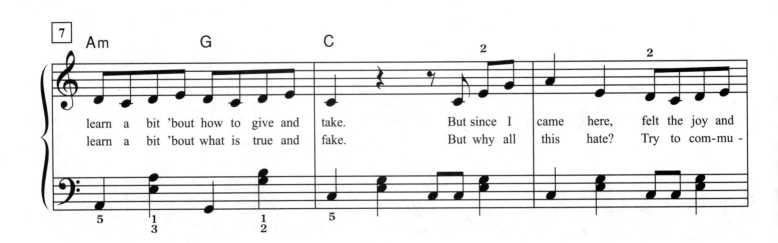

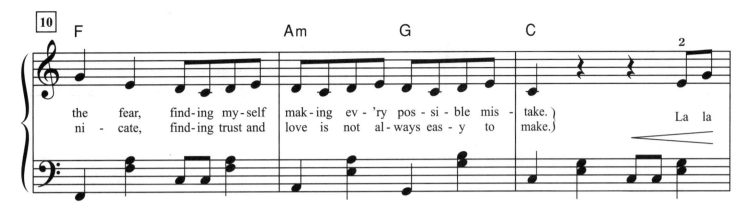

the fear, find-ing my-self mak-ing ev-'ry pos-si-ble mis - take.)
ni - cate, find-ing trust and love is not al-ways eas-y to make.)
La la

la la, la la la la la la, la la la la la,— la la la,— la la

la. La la la la, la la la la la la, la la la la

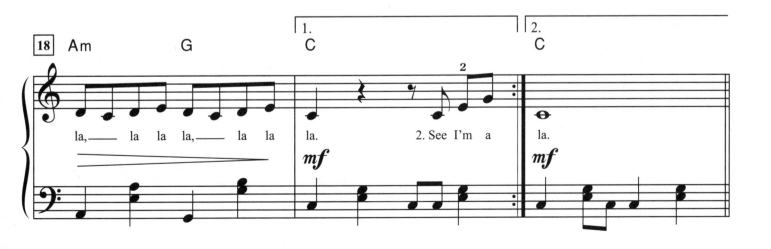

la,— la la la,— la la la. 2. See I'm a la.

Bridge:

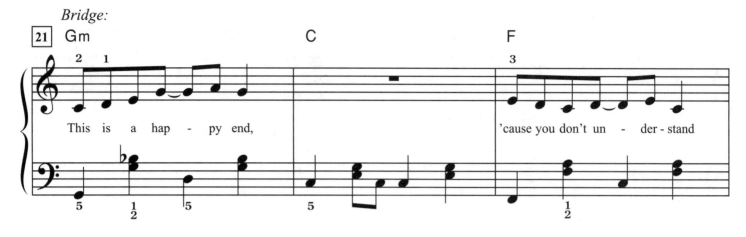

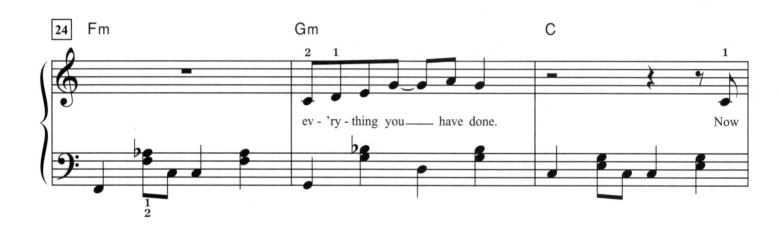

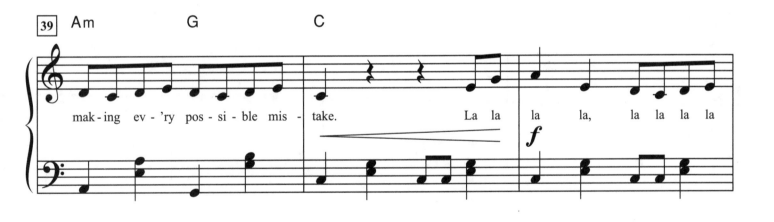

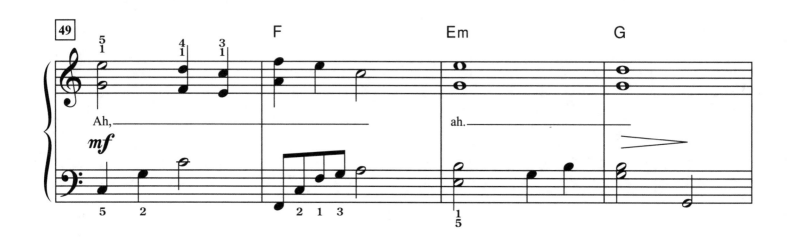

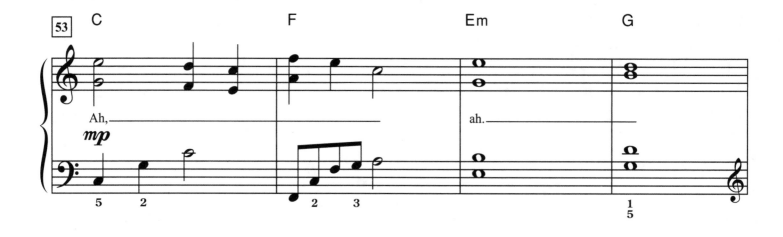

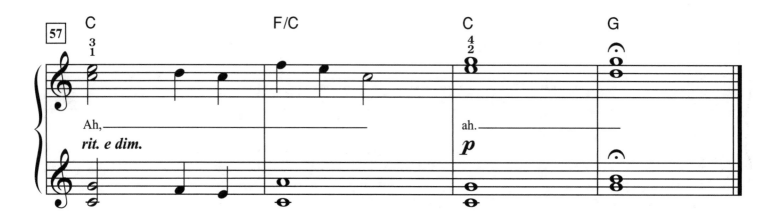

THE NOTEBOOK
(MAIN TITLE)

Based on the 1996 best-selling novel by Nicholas Sparks, the 2004 film *The Notebook* has become a standard romantic film. It features Ryan Gosling, Rachel McAdams, James Garner and Gena Rowlands in a story that spans six decades. Aaron Zigman's score features this main theme, which tenderly portrays the tribulations of love.

Written by Aaron Zigman
Arranged by Dan Coates

Slowly, with expression

THE REASON

"The Reason" is California-based rock band Hoobastank's biggest single to date. Released in December of 2003, it reached number two on the Billboard Hot 100 and number one on the Modern Rock Tracks charts. It earned a Grammy nomination for Song of the Year and was featured in the final episode of the television show *Friends*.

Words and Music by Daniel Estrin and Douglas Robb
Arranged by Dan Coates

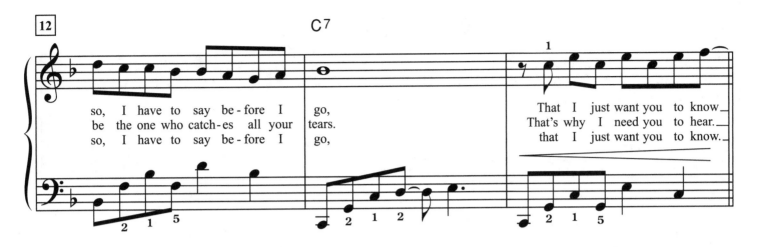

so, I have to say be-fore I go, / That I just want you to know_
be the one who catch-es all your tears. / That's why I need you to hear._
so, I have to say be-fore I go, / that I just want you to know._

Chorus:

I've found a rea - son for me___ to

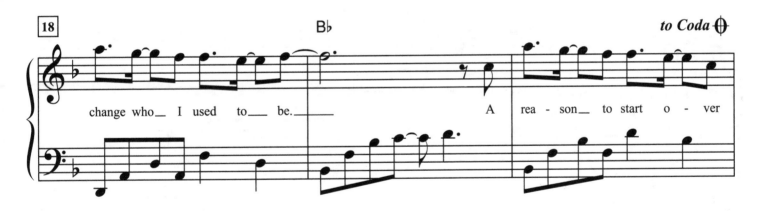

change who_ I used to_ be.___ A rea - son_ to start o - ver

to Coda

1.

new, and the rea - son_ is you. 2. I'm

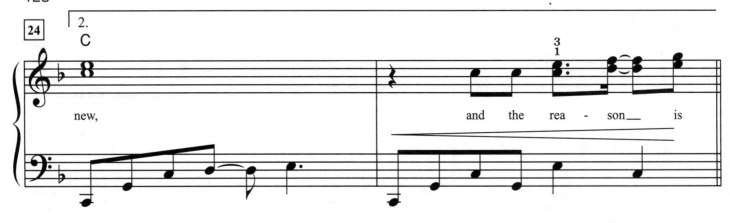

new,

and the rea - son__ is

Bridge:

f

you,

and the rea - son__ is   you.

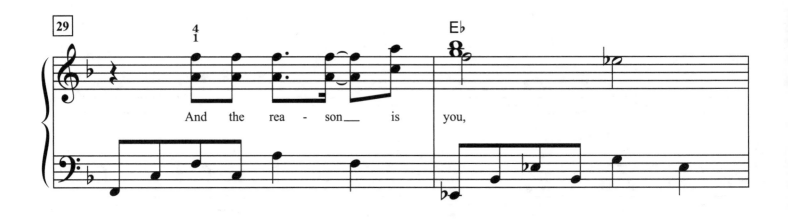

And   the   rea - son__   is   you,

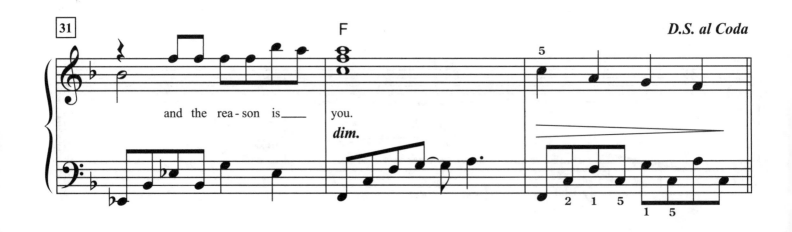

D.S. al Coda

and the rea - son is__   you.

dim.

new,   and the rea - son is_____

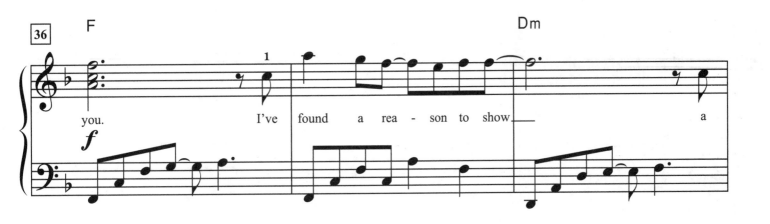

you.   I've found a rea - son to show____   a

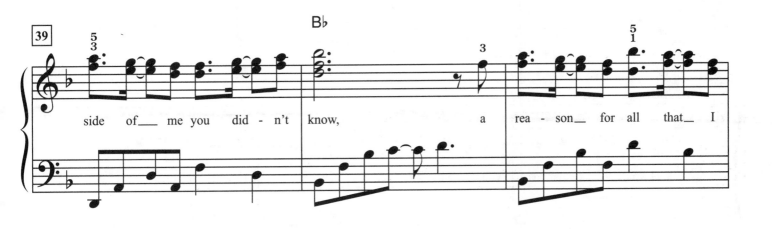

side of__ me you did - n't know,   a rea - son__ for all that__ I

do,   and the rea - son is   you.

TO WHERE YOU ARE

This single appeared on Josh Groban's 2001 self-titled debut album. The California-born Groban quickly rose to fame in 1999 when he was a stand-in for Andrea Bocelli who was to rehearse with Celine Dion for a performance of "The Prayer" at the Grammy Awards. Soon after, Groban sang at the inauguration of California governor Gray Davis, appeared on the television show *Ally McBeal*, and his career skyrocketed.

Words and Music by Richard Marx and Linda Thompson
Arranged by Dan Coates

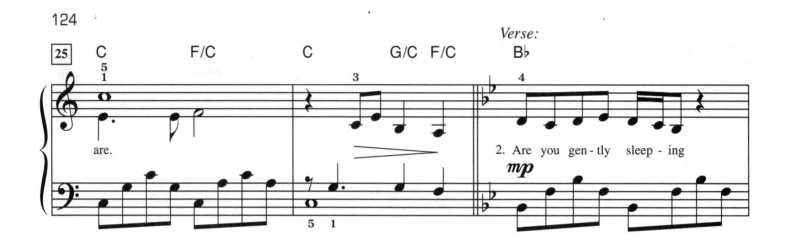

D.S. al Coda

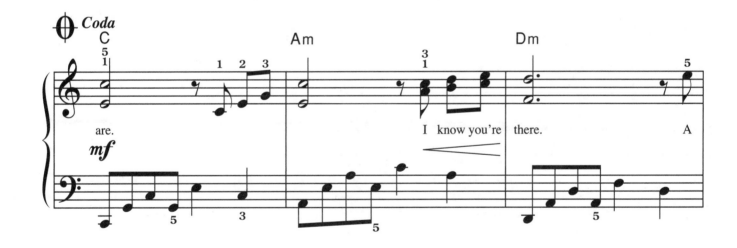

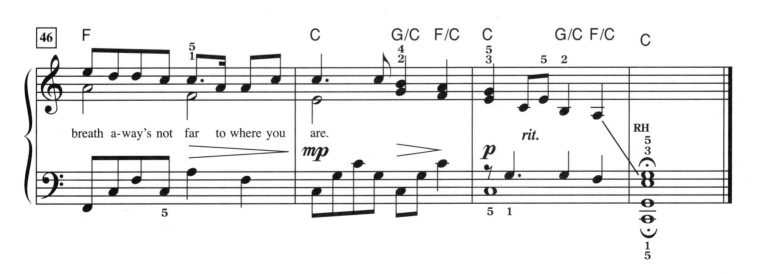

THIS I PROMISE YOU

The popular boy band N*SYNC had a worldwide hit with "This I Promise You" from their 2000 album *No Strings Attached*. The single held solid places on both the Billboard Hot 100 and Adult Contemporary charts. N*SYNC was formed in 1995 under the guidance of boy band impresario Lou Pearlman. Since going on a temporary hiatus in 2002, only Justin Timberlake has achieved success with a solo career.

Words and Music by Richard Marx
Arranged by Dan Coates

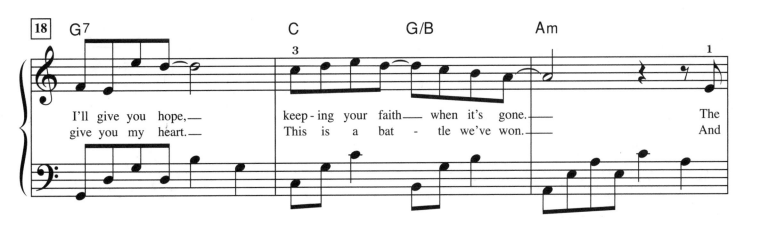

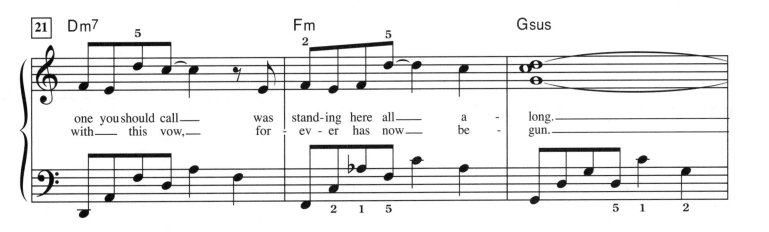

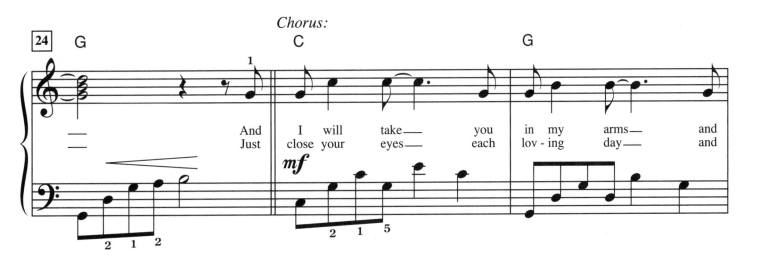

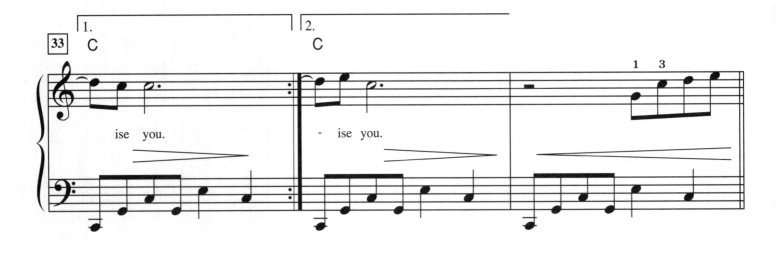

With-out you in my life, ba - by, I just

would - n't be liv - ing at all._____ And

Chorus:

I will take___ you each
close your eyes___ you

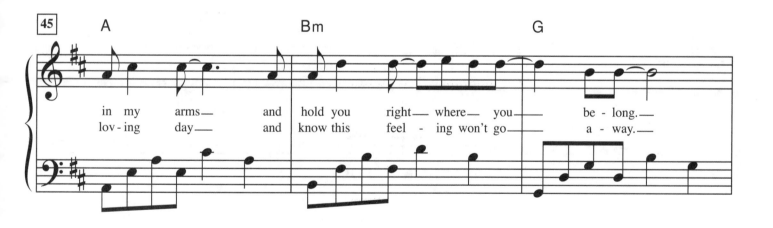

in my arms___ and hold you right___ where___ you___ be - long.___
lov - ing day___ and know this feel - ing won't go___ a - way.___

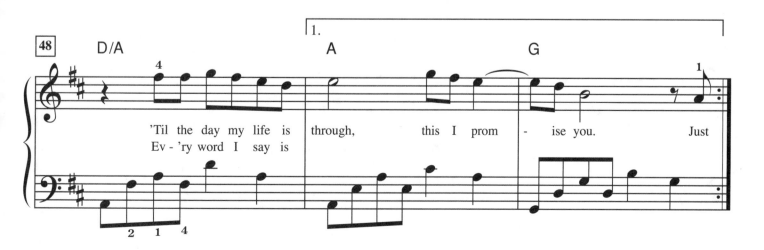

1.

'Til the day my life is through, this I prom - ise you. Just
Ev - 'ry word I say is

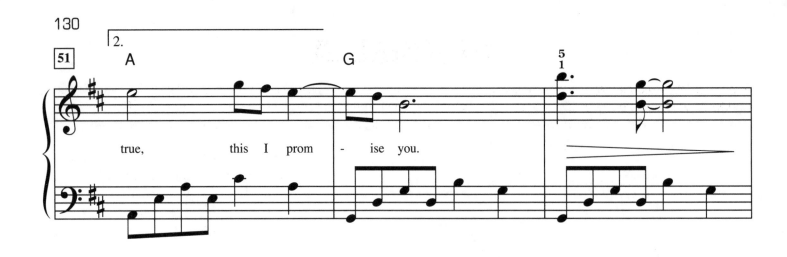

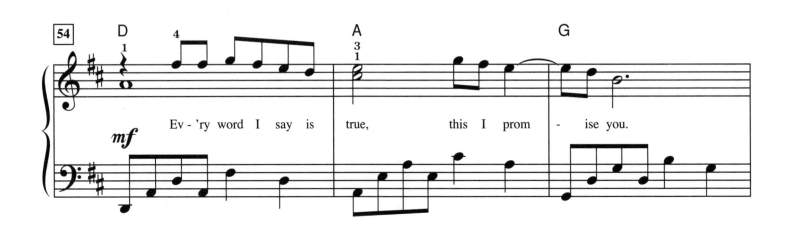

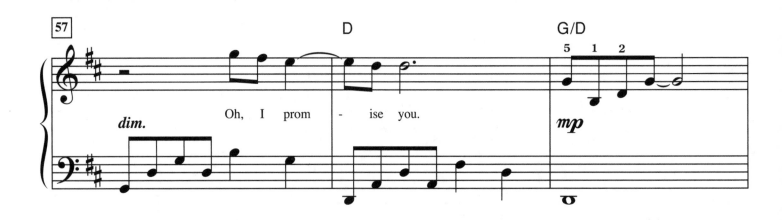

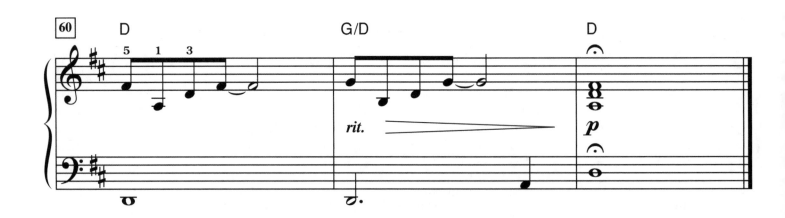

UMBRELLA

Rihanna collaborated with rap superstar Jay-Z on this hit single from her third album *Good Girl Gone Bad*. "Umbrella" has achieved worldwide success on the pop charts and has also been covered in a variety of styles by countless artists. In 2008 "Umbrella" won a Grammy for Best Rap/Sung Collaboration. It was also nominated for Record of the Year and Song of the Year.

Words and Music by Terius Nash, Shawn Carter,
Thaddis Harrell and Christopher Stewart
Arranged by Dan Coates

Moderately, with a steady beat

WAKE ME UP WHEN SEPTEMBER ENDS

"Wake Me Up When September Ends" is the fourth single from Green Day's seventh studio album, *American Idiot*. Lead singer Billie Joe Armstrong wrote this song as a tribute to his father, who passed away when Armstrong was 10 years old. The other hit single from *American Idiot*, "Boulevard of Broken Dreams," is on page 22.

Words by Billie Joe Music by Green Day
Arranged by Dan Coates

YOU RAISE ME UP

Josh Groban's version of "You Raise Me Up" was featured on his second album, 2003's *Closer*, and was nominated for a Grammy award. Though Groban is oft-associated with this single, it was written by Rolf Løvland and Brendan Graham of the New Age group Secret Garden and performed on their album *Once in a Red Moon* (released March, 2002) by Irish singer-songwriter Brian Kennedy.

Words and Music by Rolf Løvland and Brendan Graham
Arranged by Dan Coates

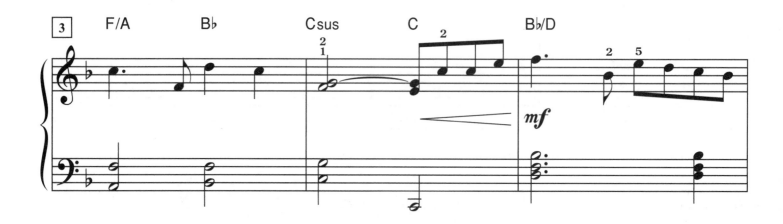

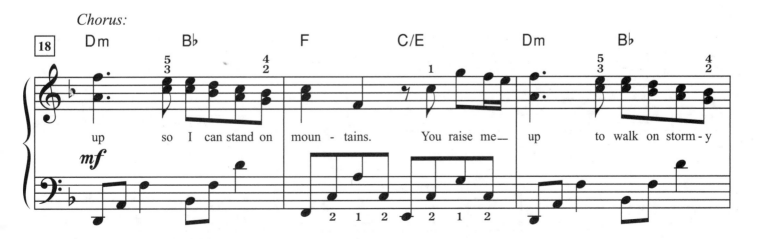

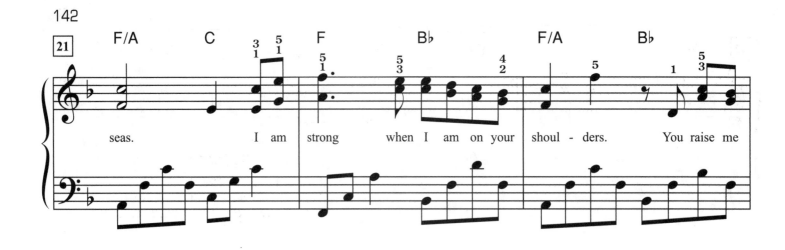

seas.   I am   strong   when I   am on your   shoul - ders.   You raise me

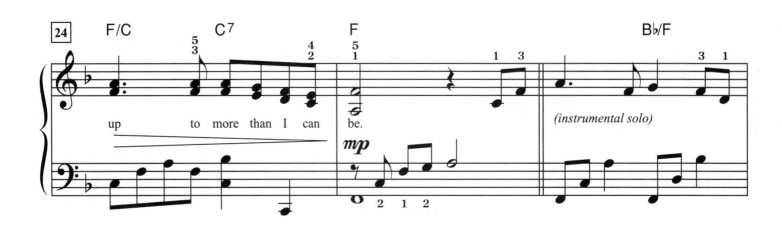

up   to more than I   can   be.

(instrumental solo)

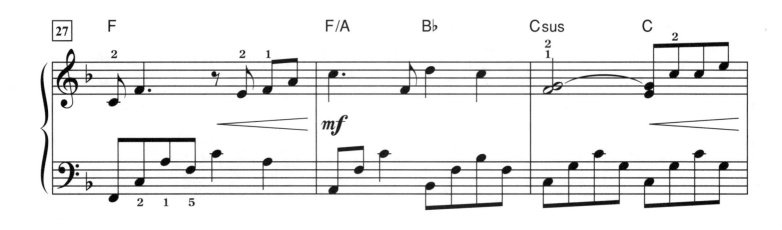

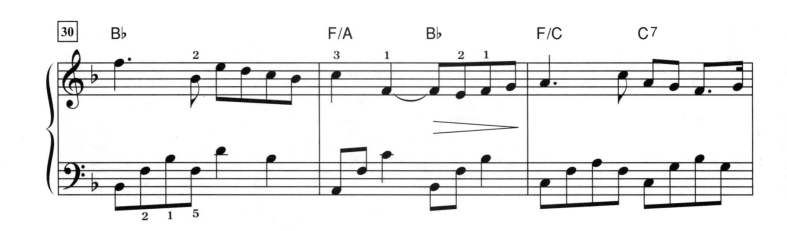

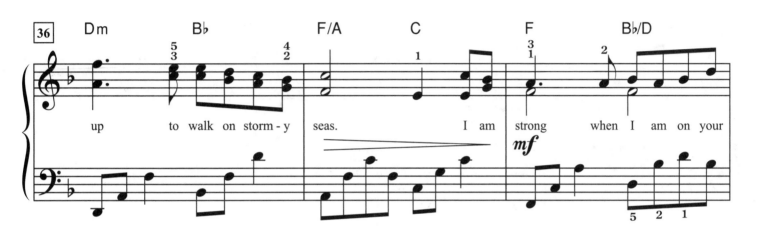

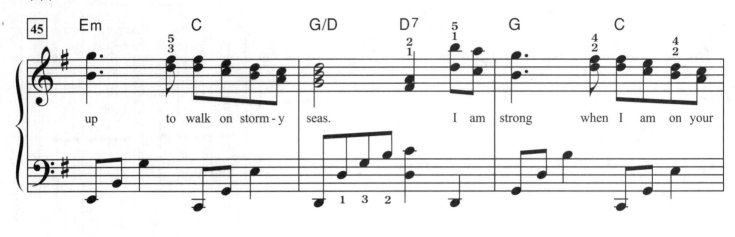

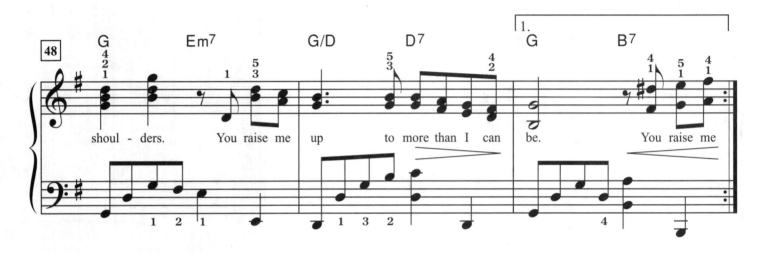

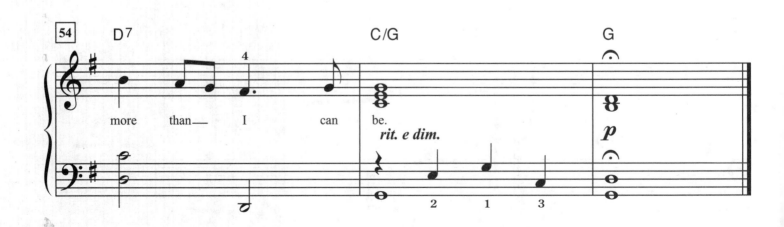